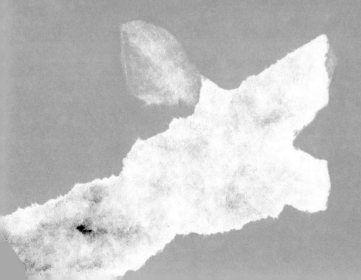

BOOKS BY MICHAEL J. ARLEN
Living-Room War
Exiles
An American Verdict

AN AMERICAN VERDICT

AN
AMERICAN
VERDICT

MICHAEL J. ARLEN

DOUBLEDAY & COMPANY, INC., GARDEN CITY, NEW YORK
1973

ISBN: 0-385-03677-9
LIBRARY OF CONGRESS CATALOG CARD NUMBER: 73–79640
COPYRIGHT © 1973 BY MICHAEL J. ARLEN
ALL RIGHTS RESERVED
PRINTED IN THE UNITED STATES OF AMERICA
FIRST EDITION

For Alice

AN AMERICAN VERDICT

Said Sergeant Groth: "We tried our best to avoid loss of life or wounding anyone. I called on our men to stop shooting, and they did. I asked the other people to surrender, shouting that we had a search warrant, and they didn't obey. A man's voice shouted from one of the dark rooms in the place, 'Shoot it out!'—and they tried it. Our men had no choice but to return fire."

THIS morning the haze hangs low over Chicago, and above the grey haze there is a thick layer of grey cloud. Rain is in the air, and there are puddles on the street from a brief storm the night before. The lake also looks grey: Lake Michigan, which stretches nearly three hundred miles from its southern rim—a few feet from the apartment buildings on Lake Shore Drive—to its northern tip in the woods and islands of Michigan.

It is early summer, 1972, and the water is warming, although today a bit windswept. Many boats are moored in the marinas: sailboats and motor cruisers—an almost Mediterranean scene beneath the massiveness of the line of buildings. There are small waves on the lake. A few miles out, a freighter moves low in the water, on its way over to the docks in East Chicago.

Inside the city, there are the usual sounds of modern city life. Cars and buses. A jet (invisible today) grumbles its way overhead to O'Hare. Jackhammers from a building site. Especially in what is called the North side of Chicago, which is the area north of the Loop and near the lake, there has been much construction in the past twenty years. High-rise apartments. Hotels. Fancy shops. Office buildings. The immense John Hancock tower—part office building, part apartment house—now stands nearby the Drake Hotel. A mile or so south of it, the even taller Standard of Indiana building is nearly finished, and not far from there rises the giant secular shape of the new Sears building which will soon become the "world's tallest." The stockyards have been torn down. Gucci has recently opened a new shop. Likewise I. Magnin. There are plans to build a Ritz Hotel. The Lincoln Park Zoo has been redone by an architect, with flowers and glass and handsome brick. There is talk of extending the beaches farther into the lake.

In the morning haze, the traffic proceeds down Michigan Avenue, and State Street, and La Salle Street, bearing businessmen from the northern suburbs to their offices above or near the Loop. And beyond the Loop, toward the south and west—the famous South side and West side —stretches the rest of the city. Old brick buildings. Tenements. Small businesses: an immense expanse of small rundown shops and small rundown dwellings—a flat drear panorama, broken only by one or two new California-style shopping centers at the outer limits of the city; or by the cathedral mass of a nineteenth-century factory; or by the several clusters of what are called, in the New

4

Language, "low-income housing projects": Stonehenge-like gatherings of grim twenty-story buildings, the lower windows broken, the walls defaced, the grass littered with debris. The "projects," with names like Mother Cabrini and Robert Taylor Homes, stand apart from their surroundings, as if somehow abandoned to the present tenants by some long-vanished occupying force which has since returned home (or has perfected the art of building elsewhere), and often appear in fact to have been separated from the rest of the city by the concrete interlacings of the great expressways which Chicago has built to connect itself to the suburbs. Near Mother Cabrini, a tall cyclone fence surrounds a lumber yard. A patrol car stands on a side street. On the paper-strewn grass, a half-dozen black kids play at stickball.

ON the seventh floor of the Cook County courthouse, in Room 702, which is Judge Philip Romiti's courtroom, the court is in session. Judge Romiti, a thin man with an angular face, a dark fringe of hair, sits at the bench—his head resting lightly against one hand. On a long wood table below him are arrayed a variety of weapons: shotguns, rifles, revolvers. The courtroom is crowded: three benches of press, and several dozen spectators, many of them black. There is no jury. On the Judge's right there are four tables for the defendants and their lawyers: eleven defendants and seven lawyers. On the prosecution's side there are two smaller tables and four men. And beside them, tilted at an angle, its top removed—a bit like one of those large, expensive dollhouses at Schwarz—is a grey-painted plywood model of the interior of an apartment.

On the witness stand sits a black woman. She seems in her twenties—and large, square-shouldered, with a smooth, tough face. Her hair is in an Afro style. A lawyer stands directly below the Judge. He holds a shotgun in his hand. "I am holding Exhibit 13-F," he says in a flat, almost conversational voice, "and I am going to ask you if, in the period between October and December, 1969, you have ever seen this weapon?"

The black woman at the witness stand stares disinterestedly toward the lawyer, toward the shotgun; looks away for a moment, for a long moment—she appears to be thinking, or dreaming, or maybe nothing (the pause is now long, and longer). "I don't recollect," she says finally.

The lawyer continues to hold the weapon. "You don't recollect seeing it? Or you don't recollect whether or not you saw it?"

The woman again looks toward him. From the side, her face somehow seems less smooth, less female. "I don't recollect whether or not," she says.

The lawyer puts down the shotgun, picks up another weapon—this time a carbine. "I am now holding Exhibit 23-C," he intones in the same flat voice, "and I am going to ask you if, in the period between October and December, 1969, you have ever seen this weapon?"

The lawyer's name is Thomas Sullivan, and he is lawyer for the defense. He is considered to be a good young lawyer—forty-two years old, Irish, works for a prominent Chicago law firm. Some years back he acquired a kind of civil liberties reputation here for representing a university

7

professor against the House Un-American Activities Committee.

The case today is not what one would ordinarily call a civil liberties case. Officially, its title is: *No. 71, CR 1791. People of the State of Illinois, Plaintiff, vs. Edward V. Hanrahan, et al., Defendants.*

Edward V. Hanrahan is seated at the largest of the defendants' tables, and in the chair nearest the bench. He wears a dark, almost black suit, and has dark close-cut hair. He sits turned in his chair so as to face the witness—in fact seems the only one of the defendants to be paying close attention. His left hand rests on the table, lightly tapping on a pad of yellow paper. His right hand is clenched just below his chin.

Edward Hanrahan is State's Attorney of Cook County —an office roughly equivalent to District Attorney elsewhere, only here the district is the most populous county in Illinois, the county which contains Chicago. The State's Attorney of Cook County (which is an elective office) is the branch of Chicago government which indicts, or does not indict; which prosecutes, or does not prosecute. It is an important job, and two hundred attorneys work under him. At present, he is charged—along with one Assistant State's Attorney, several police officials, and five policemen—with a "conspiracy to obstruct justice" in connection with a raid, conducted by his office, on an apartment at 2337 West Monroe Street, in the early morning hours of December 4, 1969, in which several members of the Black Panther Party were wounded, and two officials of the Black Panther Party were killed.

Tom Sullivan, still holding the carbine, is now saying:

8

"You don't recollect seeing it? Or you don't recollect whether or not you saw it?"

The woman does not bother to look up, or to look anywhere. "I don't recollect whether or not," she says.

A PUBLIC-SPIRITED morning in City Hall: inside the motel-Mussolini, wood-paneled, carpeted, airport-chapel grandeurs of the new City Council chamber, Mayor Daley addresses several hundred "civic leaders" on the subject of police-community relations. There are some ministers in the audience. Some bankers. The publisher of the Field newspapers sits in the back, not with the press. There are a few blacks, such as Claude Holman, who is the Mayor's chief black representative on the City Council. Mostly there are Democratic aldermen, and Cook County officeholders.

"The Police Department serves and protects the citizen," says the Mayor. "The citizen looks to the Police Department for protection. There should be no interference with police protection."

"In other cities," says the Mayor, "citizens stand by and see people murdered and raped."

And: "Chicago has one of the lowest crime rates of any city."

And: "The police are just as human as you and I. Nobody wants brutality—but should a policeman be called a brute? A pig? An S.O.B.? Should a policeman stand there unmoved? I don't think that I would take it if that person called my mother one of those appellations."

And: "The bad image of the policeman is a triumph of propaganda and falsification. In many cases, the TV people will just put a brick in a man's hand."

And: "The Lord knows how long I'm going to be the leader of this great city."

And: "Our great problem can be summed up in one word—lack of communication."

There is loud applause. A sharply dressed black man called Erwin France, who is in charge of the Mayor's "model cities" program, speaks briefly on the subject of brotherhood and cooperation between "all citizens of any color or persuasion." Four Deputy Police Superintendents are introduced. More applause. A young woman in bluejeans rises, announces that she has a question on behalf of the lesbian women of Chicago. The Mayor moves warily toward the microphone. The woman asks her question, which she reads solemnly from a notebook, about mistreatment of women. The amphitheater is silent. The Mayor stands by the microphone. The four Deputy Superintendents are behind him. He looks out into the audience. Just then a man in a brown suit stands up. He is Spanish or Mexican, and says there is not enough Spanish-American representation on the Mayor's police-community board. "Thank you," the Mayor says. He quickly turns from the microphone. Several of the senior functionaries and aldermen get up. The Mayor's meeting is adjourned.

Verlina Brewer said: "Then they just kept on shooting and finally I don't know how long they shot in, but it was for a pretty long time and finally, you know, we were all hurt pretty bad, and I don't remember what we said, but anyway the police were still shooting, and then they kicked the door open, you know, and started going out to the dining room, and then out to the kitchen, and I can't remember exactly who went first, except that I got up and went in the kitchen, and people were laying on the floor."

ONCE it was hog butcher to the nation. Railroad center: The Great Northern. The Burlington & Quincy. The Chicago & Eastern. The Chicago & Milwaukee. The Rock Island. The Colorado & Southern. The Gulf, Mobile & Ohio. The Louisville & Nashville. The Soo Line. The Rio Grande . . . Here was the link between the East—the moneyed, Europe-eyeing East—and the remote, large promises of California. Here McCormick built his reaper. Here William Jenney devised and built the first skyscraper: the Home Insurance building—ten stories tall, "constructed of steel girders, hung with a curtain of light masonry, and with bands of horizontally set windows." From Chicago, Sears and Roebuck sent out their first catalogues. Timber was brought in from Michigan and

Wisconsin. The boats carried ore down from Lake Superior. They called it a "building place." Once, nearly the whole town burned down—a town of wood shacks and mud. In two years they built it up again in brick and stone.

Today, Chicago is still the business center of the country, and still a place of building—and of building scandals. For a while it was the "second city" after New York. Now, after New York and Los Angeles, it is the third largest city in North America. Three cities: a triumvirate. Los Angeles is sometimes said to represent our future— condominiums and cars and drive-ins and magnetic-tape factories. New York is harder to place: it is either dead or dying, snarled in strikes and taxes, or else all aglitter— the "communications" center, the place where hit shows open, where Walter Cronkite works, where Leonard Bernstein lives, where Jacqueline Onassis hires her cooks; perhaps our confused present.

And Chicago? Surely not our past? The huge construction cranes crank and rattle throughout the day. Ever larger ore boats cross the lake. The hotels are filled with businessmen on convention. The railroads are no longer so busy or numerous, here or anywhere, but O'Hare is now celebrated as the "nation's busiest airport." Now, too, there is a first-rate art museum and a fine symphony. There are brand-new condominiums of glass and steel beside the lake. There are drive-ins off State Street which play rock music into the night. There are girls in blue-jeans, and long-haired boys on Italian bicycles. There are Porsches in the parking lots, and crowds of young

15

men and women—"singles"—at the big bar in the Playboy Towers.

A modern city. Be not too deceived, although there
are high-rises here just as in Santa Monica or New York.
And sports cars. And new expressways. There are girls
in bluejeans everywhere. Chicago today seems no more
a part of any triumvirate than it ever was. The other two
great cities, with their flash, and ego drives, and ambig-
uous sexuality, are perhaps the two Romes of our modern
empire. Chicago, notwithstanding its appearance of being
an accommodating midpoint between the two, remains
the Ancient Capital.

Look upon its brick and stone, which stretch like a sea
around the scattered high-rises. Look upon its citizen-
businessmen, male and purposive as astronauts. Chicago
is the serious city of America, the city which still most
goes about the main business of America, which—despite
McLuhan, the Counter-Culture, and the supposed failure
of the Old Order—still seems to be business, trade, trans-
port, commerce, money; and goes about it steadfastly,
with scant doubt as to the point of the undertaking, and
with all the old energies and pieties intact.

Look at the smoke from the mills in East Chicago. Look
upon the shoppers in the Loop. It may well be that rich
ladies here do their shopping in New York, or wish they
did, and that young people with movie cameras, type-
writers, dreams of acting, or new political ideas, look out
from here across the flat dry center of the country toward
the ocean breezes of both coasts, the ocean glitter. But
it should be said that this flat center of the country is still
a considerable empire, and that Chicago is its capital.

Hemingway and Ben Hecht and Bobby Hull, and many others, may have noisily left it—Bobby Hull, as people say here, was always Canadian. Watch instead the busloads of schoolchildren from downstate lined up outside the elevators of the John Hancock building. Watch the alumni gather for the annual dinner of the De LaSalle Institute, the big Catholic high school, where mayors and precinct captains and salesmen and policemen have gone —a heavy grey building, great pieces of grey stone, and athletic trophies in rows of glass cases. Nuns and Brothers in the corridors. Grey stone.

Outside now, this afternoon, in the distance on Lake Michigan (the water a light blue) there are sailboats all in a row: a boat race. The sun shines through the clouds. White boats and colored sails—a handsome sight. It is another view of the Ancient Capital—a tableau of white boats and colored sails, perhaps painted by a traveling artist on one of the walls, on one of the brick or stone walls.

And in Room 702 of the Cook County courthouse, Thomas Sullivan puts down the last of the firearms, turns back toward the witness stand. "And when you went out of that room," he asks, "did you think Fred Hampton was dead?"

Deborah Johnson picks up the microphone again. "I thought he was dead," she says.

AT around six in the morning of December 4, 1969, the bodies of Fred Hampton and Matt Clark were brought by police from the apartment at 2337 West Monroe to the Cook County Morgue. Hampton, twenty-one years old, had been head of the Black Panther Party in Illinois. Matt Clark, twenty-two years old, was a Panther Party member from downstate in Peoria. Four Panther members, who had been wounded in the raid, were in Cook County Hospital. Three others who had been in the apartment were in Cook County Jail. All seven were charged with attempted murder, armed violence, and unlawful possession of weapons.

LATER that morning, at around nine-thirty, the following statement was issued by State's Attorney Hanrahan:

This morning, pursuant to a search warrant, State's Attorney's police attempted to search the first floor apartment at 2337 West Monroe Street to seize sawed-off shotguns and other illegal weapons stored there. Our office had reliable information that this location was a depot for illegal weapons gathered by members of the Black Panther Party.

As soon as Sergeant Daniel Groth and Officer James Davis, leading our men, announced their office, occupants of the apartment attacked them with shotgun fire. The officers immediately took cover. The occupants continued firing at our policemen from several rooms within the apartment.

Thereafter, three times Sergeant Groth ordered all his men to cease firing and told the occupants to come out with their hands up. Each time, one of the occupants replied, "Shoot it out," and they continued firing at the police officers. Finally, the occupants threw down their guns and were arrested.

The immediate violent criminal reaction of the occupants in shooting at announced police officers emphasizes the extreme viciousness of the Black Panther Party. So does their refusal to cease firing at the police officers when urged to do so several times. Fortunately only one police officer was wounded. We wholeheartedly commend the police officers for their bravery, their remarkable restraint, and their discipline in the face of this Black Panther attack—as should every decent citizen in the community.

The four Chicago newspapers for the most part received the State's Attorney's statement without demurrer. "PANTHER CHIEF, AIDE, KILLED IN GUN BATTLE WITH POLICE," said the *Daily News* in a big headline, and then went on to quote Hanrahan's statement and to interview some of the raiding policemen. "Sergeant Daniel Groth gave this account: 'I knocked on the door. Someone inside said "Who's there?" I announced I was a police officer and had a search warrant. There was no response. We pushed in the front door. As we entered, a girl lying on a bed fired a blast from a shotgun at us.'" Detectives Edward Carmody and John Ciszewiski were quoted as saying that a man, "later identified as Hampton, had fired at them with a shotgun and pistol from the rear room." A reporter for the "Noon News" on WMAQ (the NBC affiliate) then obtained an interview with Bobby Rush, the No. 2 Panther in Illinois—with whom Hampton normally shared the Monroe Street apartment. Standing on the steps of the raided apartment, and filmed by TV cameras, Rush said that "Hampton was murdered in his sleep."

Within a few minutes after the program was over, Hanrahan telephoned the news manager at WMAQ and demanded a public retraction from the station, as well as the complete tapes of the Rush interview. The news manager said no to both requests. Hanrahan then called a press conference for later that afternoon. At the conference, all the firearms and ammunition which the police had taken from the Panther apartment were displayed on a large table. The contents of one box of bullets had been emptied and the individual bullets had been stood in rows, tip upward. Twenty-six different weapons had been seized in the apartment, including four shotguns, and nearly ten thousand rounds of ammunition. Hanrahan repeated his view that the gun battle had been a "vicious attack on officers of the law."

On the day after the shooting, hundreds of people, mostly black, came to walk through the apartment at

West Monroe Street, which curiously had not been sealed by the police. It was not the first gun battle in Chicago, nor the first shoot-out between the police and black activists, but Fred Hampton had seemed to many to have been a different sort of black activist. He was young. He came from solid people—his father had worked twenty years for Corn Products in nearby Argo. Hampton had played football at Maywood High School, and while there had organized a protest for a community swimming pool. As a Panther, he spoke well, with warmth, and not always with anger.

One thing that many people now noticed was the size of the apartment—how small it was. Six tiny rooms; not more than forty feet between the front and back doors. Nine men and women had been asleep inside, scattered throughout the rooms. The size of the bedroom in which Hampton and Deborah Johnson slept—the bloodstained mattress in fact was still there, a chair, a reading lamp, the paperboard walls pocked with bullet holes—was scarcely more than ten feet by ten. There had been fourteen policemen coming in from the outside, coming in from the front and back. There had been a lot of shooting. And this was then another thing that people noticed: that the bullet holes in the walls seemed to have been made by bullets coming *in* from the outside; that most of the front windows were still intact; that there were few visible marks, if any, that might have been made by bullets going from the inside—*out*.

O<small>N</small> December 10, 1969, six days after the "shoot-out," and in response to the beginnings of editorial questioning of the event in the *Daily News* and *Sun-Times* (as well as to criticism from the NAACP and several local colleges), Hanrahan telephoned the Chicago *Tribune*, still very much an authoritative voice in Chicago, and a traditional supporter of the civic establishment and the police, and offered it his "exclusive version" of the raid. The *Tribune* accepted the offer and dispatched two reporters, Edward Lee and Robert Wiedrich, to the State's Attorney's Office. The next morning, Lee and Wiedrich's "exclusive" appeared on the front page of the *Tribune*. It gave the State's Attorney's official positioning of the policemen during the raid. It quoted Sergeant Groth and other officers as saying they had been fired upon by the Panthers. It spoke of repeated "cease fire" offers from the police, and repeated volleys of return fire from the Panthers. It described the dead Fred Hampton "lying face down on the bed with his head facing the bedroom door, through which repeated gunfire had been directed at police in the kitchen." Generally, it restated the State's Attorney's theme—of police attempting to serve a search warrant, and then being compelled to shoot back when attacked.

In addition to its assistance with the text of the story, Hanrahan's office also provided a number of photographs, which the *Tribune* ran at the same time as the Lee-Wiedrich account. Two pictures were given special prominence in the paper—each of them of a door in the Monroe Street apartment, and each of them with large holes in the doors, several of which had been circled. One caption said: "Hail of lead tore thru [sic] bathroom door in fire from opposite bedroom, according to police. This is inside view of riddled door." The other caption said: "Kitchen in flat at 2337 Monroe St., where Black Panthers fired thru door (bullet holes circled) at State's Attorney's policemen. State's Attorney Edward Hanrahan released pictures to the Tribune showing that bullets were fired from inside the secret headquarters of Black Panthers."

Reporters from the *Sun-Times*, who had since been to the apartment, pointed out that the door in the first picture was not the bathroom door, but a door to one of the bedrooms, and that the bullet holes were going in not out. And that the circled bullet holes in the second picture were in fact not bullet holes, nor holes of any kind, but heads of nails—nailheads. When challenged on this point, Hanrahan asserted that he had not in any way evaluated or captioned the photographs—he had merely furnished them to the *Tribune*. The *Tribune* declined to comment.

On the evening of the same day that the Lee-Wiedrich story, along with the nailhead photographs, were appearing in the *Tribune*, Hanrahan once again sought to convey his version of what had happened to the public. This was December 11. Hampton and Clark had been buried. The four wounded Panthers had left Cook County Hospital and were now, with the three other survivors, under indictment for attempted murder.

Earlier in the week, Hanrahan had telephoned the major Chicago television stations and had offered them an "official re-enactment" of the raid by the policemen who had taken part in it. He gave as conditions that the television stations should agree to run the re-enactment intact, without comment, and that his representatives supervise any technical editing or cutting that might be necessary. The ABC and NBC affiliate stations declined the offer; the CBS station accepted.

Thus, at 2 P.M. on December 11, a CBS television crew appeared at the State's Attorney's Office, where Hanrahan had already arranged to have constructed a plywood representation of the Monroe Street apartment, and between two and six—supervised by Assistant State's Attorney Jalovec, and with Hanrahan making a couple of brief appearances—the fourteen officers went through their re-enactment.

It required four hours, members of the CBS crew explained later, partly because some of the policemen used profanity and so sections had to be retaped, and because of the usual technical reasons, but also because several of the officers appeared to be mixed-up, or anyway forgetful, as to what they were doing, and thus needed to be rehearsed and re-rehearsed. At the point of entry into the apartment, for instance, sometimes one man went first, sometimes another. Other officers needed reminding as to which direction they had actually been facing, or turning, or firing. There was some confusion as to the calling of cease-fires. In any case, at ten that evening, a twenty-eight minute final version of the re-enactment (edited at CBS shortly before air-time, with Jalovec present) was shown over WBBM. In virtually every respect, it repeated the *Tribune* version of the event, although much more dramatically. Officer Davis could be seen crashing through the door of the apartment. Sergeant Groth, pistol in hand, described the Panther woman on the bed "pumping a shotgun." Officers Gorman and Ciszewiski described seeing "bursts of fire" coming at them from one of the bedrooms. Sergeant Groth described again his several calls for a cease-fire, and the Panther replies to "shoot it out." After the shooting was over, said Groth, the officers had gone about their business in seizing the illegal weapons, and had taken the surviving occupants into custody.

ON January 6, 1970, the Cook County Coroner appointed a Special Coroner's Inquest to look into the events of December 4th, 1969. Six "blue ribbon" jurors were chosen. Martin Gerber, a lawyer, was named as Special Coroner. The Inquest lasted twelve days, in an atmosphere of tension and official security—with as many as fifty deputy sheriffs stationed around the courtroom at various times. The Panthers, who were currently under indictment, refused to testify. The fourteen police officers testified, and gave virtually the same account of what had happened as they had given to the *Tribune* and over WBBM. A firearms examiner for the Chicago Police Department testified, and, among other things, identified three recovered shotgun shells as having been fired from a Panther weapon. On January 23, the Coroner's jury returned a verdict of "justifiable homicide."

On January 30, 1970, a Cook County Grand Jury—which had been summoned by State's Attorney Hanrahan—indicted the seven surviving Panthers for "attempted murder" and other crimes, such as "aggravated battery," and "armed violence."

Said the indictment:

The Grand Jurors chosen, selected, and sworn, in and for the County of Cook, in the State of Illinois, in the name and by the authority of the People of the State of Illinois, upon their oaths present that on December 4th, 1969, at and within said County, Brenda Harris, Verlina Brewer, Blair Anderson, Ronald Satchell, Harold Bell, Deborah Johnson, and Louis Truelock, also known as Louis Trueluck, committed the offense of attempted murder in that they, with intent to commit the offense of murder, intentionally and knowingly attempted to kill Daniel Groth, James Davis, Joseph Gorman, George Jones, Edward Carmody, Philip Joseph, Raymond Broderick, William Corbett, William Kelly, and John Ciszewiski, without lawful justification, in violation of Chapter 38, section 8-4, of the Illinois Revised Statutes, 1967, contrary to the Statute, and against the peace and dignity of the same People of the State of Illinois.

The indictments were based largely on the same testimony as had been given by the fourteen policemen at the Special Coroner's Inquest; and on the same police scientific evidence, which had identified three recovered shotgun shells from Panther weapons—two of which (the police report said) had been fired from the "Harris shotgun," the weapon supposedly held, and "pumped," and "fired," by Brenda Harris when the police came into the apartment.

On February 11, 1970, the seven Panthers pleaded not guilty.

At around the same time that the Cook County Grand Jury was listening to its evidence, and in response to "a situation of intense public concern," a Federal Grand Jury was empaneled under Jerris Leonard, then Assistant Attorney General of the United States. Ballistic experts from the FBI were called in to collect and examine the available physical evidence. Jerris Leonard made plans to come out to Chicago in March of that year and gather further testimony.

CARMODY, Broderick, Corbett, Kelly, Mulchrone . . . It's probably impossible to make sense of Chicago without knowing something about the Irish. They're certainly not the only white ethnic group here, or even the largest —for years there has been a multitude of Poles, as well as Germans and Italians and Central Europeans and just about everyone else. Mayor Cermak, a Pole, in fact, put together one of the original urban-ethnic Democratic Machines here in the early Thirties. Annunzio, Scariano, Rostenkowski, Kucharowski—these are all familiar sounds in Chicago politics today.

But the principal civic sounds seem to be Irish. Dick Daley—Mayor for the past twenty years. Before him it was Ed Kelly. And before Kelly it was Kennelly. Tom

Keane is Daley's emissary on the City Council. The County Board President is George Dunne. The Fire Commissioner's name is Quinn. The Circuit Clerk's name is Danaher. The Cardinal's name is Cody. The Superintendent of Police is Jim Conlisk, who is the son of old Jim Conlisk, a former Assistant Superintendent of Police. The State's Attorney is Edward Vincent Hanrahan.

To look at the names of city officials in this country since the nineteenth century, you'd think that the Irish were the only people to come here since the Pilgrims, and that directly after landing they headed straight for City Hall. It's true they arrived in enormous numbers, especially in the second part of the last century, and what comes through even in reading about the great Irish famines is that here once again was a huge shaping force —a force that we ourselves have no felt knowledge of— played out upon another people: in this instance a white, kindred-seeming people, but perhaps one that may nearly always remain slightly alien from those of us who did not once experience such an event.

And unlike, it seems, so many of the other peoples who came here—the Scots and English who went to farm New England, the Germans and Scandinavians and Central Europeans who went to farm the middle west—the Irish went mainly to the cities, and remained there. Boston. New York. Jersey City. Philadelphia. Eventually, Chicago. The first urban American slum-dwellers—although shanties they were then quaintly called, shanty-dwellers.

They stayed in the cities, and did the menial work. Day laborers. Housemaids. In this, the Irish had the advantage of language over most of the other immigrants.

They also had the advantage of an instinct for politics, which had been developed over centuries of reacting to British rule, and in some cases of actual embryonic political organizations, which had traveled with them. By the early years of the twentieth century, the American Irish controlled the Roman Catholic Church in America. And for the most part they also controlled the inner-working, the power apparat, of the majority of the larger cities in the country, most certainly including Chicago.

All those leagues, and political organizations, and Social & Athletic clubs—looking back on them from the present, with its remaining Democratic Machines (either tottering or stonelike) or with the new synthetic tribalism that seeks to replace them (Black Athletes for Nixon, Polish Computer Programmers for Agnew), the Irish political intrusion into American life seems to have been wondrously alive and familial. Members of the tribe were provided jobs. Work. *Patronage.* The tribe continued the tribe's elect in whatever high office the tribe's elect had managed to scramble to. It is not all that different in Chicago today.

American cities, especially those inland, away from the Atlantic, must have seemed dark and remote places for Europeans to inhabit, even one hundred years ago. Communities of Poles, and Irish, and Swedes, and Germans scattered and huddled and moving across an openness that nobody yet had quite measured, at least imaginatively; and within each community, *the family*—the source of life, and food, and warmth; the definer of life.

"Studs left home immediately after breakfast so he could get away from the old lady. She was always pes-

32

tering him, telling him to pray and ask God if he had a vocation. And maybe she'd have wanted him to go to the store, beat rugs, or clean the basement out. He didn't feel like being a janitor. He would work, but he wouldn't be a janitor." This from James Farrell's *Studs Lonigan,* about life on Chicago's South side, first published in 1932. Working-class Irish, sheltering in cities under the secular umbrella of the Irish precinct captain, and under the spiritual umbrella of the Irish priest. Close-knit. Tribal. My friend is with me, mine enemy is against me. Ambition. Fear of God. Fear. Some of the strongest, most moving writing in the world has been the literature of escape, and certainly some of the best of that has been written by grown Irish children, by Joyce and O'Neil and also Farrell, about the attempted escapes from these tribal earth-families, about trying to escape from being forever defined by these definers of life.

It's hard, especially for an outsider, a comfortable American too, to have much of a real sense of this today. Ethnicity, we are told it is, as if that made it any easier to feel. The contents of the proverbial melting-pot appear nearly blended, or (as we are sometimes told) never quite existed. By now we are aware of, we more or less accept, Jews and Jewishness as a certified part of the nation and the national consciousness. There is a Jewish branch, at the very least, of the American novel. Leonard Bernstein conducts his *Mass* at the Kennedy Center. We are also, by now, thunderously aware of blacks. We may not choose to live with them, and will apparently do nearly anything to avoid having our children go to school with them, but we are most definitely aware of their presence. The colleges now teach Black Studies. There is a new Black American Novel.

There appear to be no Irish Studies program in any college, and no demand for them, although a group did assemble last year in New York to try to do something for Irish-American Culture, which so far is more a measure of what hasn't been done, what hasn't been thought to be done. And as to the Irish problem, which is to say the American Irish problem, the problem of the alienation and ostracism of the Irish in America, of the conflict between the American Irish and the nativists—there is no such Irish problem, is there? Look at the Kennedys. President John. Old Joe Kennedy. Rose. One supposes not—there is no Irish problem any more, at least not the way there used to be. An Irish Catholic has become President—the grandson of a Boston-Irish politician in the White House.

If there was a time (and there was) when the American Irish were the objects of discrimination and ostracism and exploitation—all those abstract Latinisms that have since been polished up for other causes—doubtless the rise to power, and acceptance of the Kennedys marked a figurative end to a lot of it. Still, it's worth remembering that young John Kennedy, son of Joseph, grandson of Honey-Fitz, not only was elected by the smallest of margins, but after a campaign where he had gone to some pains to dilute both his Irishness and his Catholicism. And it hadn't been that long before, in 1928, that another able man, Governor Al Smith of New York, was refused the Presidency, largely for being Irish and Catholic.

The point is perhaps—admittedly an obvious one—that

34

different peoples doubtless carry different deep memories within them, memories of things they often don't know they remember. And although today, as in most western technocracies, we are embarked on a course of gradual assimilation-of-differences, of homogeneity, of mass markets, and of standard "looks," and increasingly standard speech patterns, and increasingly standard social responses, so that things more and more have the appearance of being similar, and are increasingly described, criticized, analyzed as being similar, *the same,* everything-looks-the-same—it's probably true that we are nowhere near to that point of *sameness* as our unparticularizing eyes and ears keep telling us.

Airport terminals. Automobiles. Girls' hairdos. Expressways. Television comedies. The same, and not the same. That man standing at the bar, with his smooth face that could be from anywhere in this country, and his voice which could be from anywhere—it's true that he is classifiable in an "income group," or in a "voting bloc," and that generalities are written on the surface of his skin. But what is written inside him, where even he usually can't read it, except that now and then he moves on "impulses," on fears, on angers unaccountable by what he feels on the outside even of his mind?

It is said that the American Irish problem is over, has disappeared, has evaporated into the glow of success, of social mobility, education, less hidebound religious teaching, less oppressive families. Are *all* the descendants of Eugene O'Neil and Studs Lonigan then standing in country-club blazers at Playboy Clubs across the land, with smooth faces, accentless voices, good jobs in suburban electronics firms? It doesn't seem very likely, although some have certainly arrived there, and others are on their way.

For the present, one imagines, the American Irish are much with us—as Americans, with the inner markings from that particular experience, and as Irish, with what that faroff but even more particular experience still means. Hard-working. Political. Ambitious—and so often somehow bent low beneath the gaze, or glare, of surely one of the strictest and ungentlest notions of the Christian Deity.

"They have so behaved themselves that their kind now comprises 75% of our criminals, and has committed fully 75% of the crimes of violence among us, and the system of universal suffrage in our large cities has fallen into discredit through their incapacity for self-government." This from an editorial about the Irish in *Harper's Magazine* in 1874. One wonders, for instance, what General Robert E. Lee thought (if anything) about such matters then; or what his newly freed slaves thought of the new Irish—and vice versa. In any event, the road from then to now, from there to here, has doubtless been both longer and shorter than people who have not traveled it can well imagine; and some of the memories of the trip must have been nearly impossible to lose.

Brenda Harris said: "The other policemen— they were saying back and forth: 'There's some over here, get them.' And then another said: 'I think there is one over back there, get him.' And he kept shooting until I guess he figured, you know, everybody was dead, and then he stopped, and then while he was shooting I heard one of the occupants back in the back say: 'Don't shoot any more.' But they kept on shooting."

TWO MEETINGS

Policemen's Recognition Night: The cavernous, dark auditorium at McCormick Place is filled to the top balconies—perhaps ten thousand people. Many policemen in their best uniforms; also wives and children—some of the wives wearing corsages, the children looking freshly scrubbed. Also hundreds of city employees. A group of post office workers, who say they were let out early for the occasion, stand drinking coffee in one of the corridors. "I don't want to miss Bob Hope," one of them says. The audience is mostly white, but up in the top balconies there are several hundred black children—row after row. Down on stage, a rabbi reads aloud the Twenty-Third Psalm, while the names and badge numbers of the seventy-three policemen who were killed last year are flashed up on a screen behind him. Police Superintendent James Conlisk appears on stage, replacing the rabbi. Conlisk—large-chested, Irish, himself the son of a policeman—has the build and voice and (with his spectacles) the deceptively scholarly appearance of a high-school football coach. "We have a great show for you tonight!" says the Police Superintendent. "We will be honoring many brave and dedicated men!" Mayor Richard Daley appears on stage, walks out to the microphone. Much cheering. "No one has been maligned more than the policeman," says Mayor Daley. "No one is more deserving of respect! I am proud of the Chicago Police Department. We have no apologies to make to anyone. Oh sure we're human—but we have the finest police force in the world!" The huge audience stands and applauds. "Lately there have been complaints from various sources," the Mayor continues vaguely. "There are always people around to complain." Then, loudly: "We're not perfect. Nobody is perfect. The press isn't perfect. But if we have made mistakes, we will remedy them. We will remedy them with *love*." The Mayor is now alone on the vast stage, a small blue-suited figure standing behind a lectern, lit with spotlights—his face impassive, his voice cold and angry. "I say to you—the day we can't sit down at the local station and talk over our situation with a policeman, we're in trouble." The Mayor pronounces the word policeman as "p'liceman," which is about the only quaint touch in the auditorium that moment. "A p'liceman," the Mayor says, "doesn't care about a man's color. He doesn't care if a man is black or Spanish." Then suddenly: "Men of religion ought to be talking about *respect* for the police.

We've had too much condemnation from religious leaders." Then: "It's time to start bridging the gap." As abruptly as he had arrived, the Mayor departs, turning from the lectern, seemingly in midsentence, or in mid-sequitur, striding toward the wings. Don Rickles, the comedian, now appears, carrying a stage microphone. "Before I do anything else," he says, "I want to thank you, police officers, for making this country strong and safe." Applause. Rickles tells three jokes about being Jewish. Then he tells a joke about a black man going to heaven—giving a fine darky imitation. Then he pokes a little, a very little, discreet fun at the Mayor, who is now back in the audience. "See, the Mayor keeps nudging the guy next to him—'what's he talking about up there?'" Then Rickles says he wishes he could stay longer, but he has to leave for a stage appearance out in Niles. Police Superintendent Conlisk reappears. There are two rows of policemen now on stage behind him. Awards are given out. It is quite moving and strange. The policemen march up to Conlisk and receive from him what seem to be large bowling trophies. Investigator Hamilton receives the Carter Harrison Gold Medal. Six men receive special medals for having "exceeded the expectations of duty" in helping a boy whose arm had been accidentally lopped off—they took the boy to a hospital, explains the Superintendent, and then went back and searched for the arm, and then returned it to the boy. The winner of the Police Medal is announced: Patrolman Richard Drummond, a slim black policeman, who "while off-duty caught three men making a getaway from an armed holdup, shot one man, was shot himself and taken to hospital, and then left the hospital and identified and arrested the two remaining holdup men who were in another hospital." The two lines of policemen are marched off stage. "Left face! For'ard, march!" With the exception of Patrolman Drummond, it seems a ragtag army—no Prussian militarism here. Some of the men turn in the wrong direction. Others shuffle in and out of step. The Superintendent adds a few words. "The fine record of these fine men is sometimes lost in the noise of innuendo, gossip, and betrayal!" he says. "Sometimes," he says, "there is publicity which is detrimental to the police and to everyone in the city." The Superintendent reads a letter from President Nixon. "'Dear Superintendent Conlisk, I wish to commend you and the men of the Chicago Police Department for your outstanding job in the course of my visit on May 14th . . .'" Then a businessman who heads an organization which assists widows of policemen comes out and makes a speech. He says he knows that there are "bad apples in the barrel," but that the Superintendent has assured him that "wherever these apples are found, they will be replaced by the kind of fine men you have seen here tonight." The band strikes up. A blond singer in a long red gown and rhinestones strides across the stage. Her name is Harriet Blake. She sings a sort of spiritual, "I Want to Be Free," and then "Joy to the World," in which she tries to get the audience to join in. A local columnist, Irv Kupcinet, comes out and says that Bob Hope, the star attraction, has been delayed somewhere, but will be there soon. Miss Blake sings another song: "I Believe." A young black comedian appears, and does impersonations of Bill Cosby, John Wayne, and Hubert

41

Humphrey. Miss Blake sings "I Believe" once more. The young black comedian tells a vaguely risqué story about his boss's wife, which evokes a few scattered titters in the audience. Then: "Seriously," he says, "I want to leave you with this thought: it's character that makes the difference. Color never made a man." Applause. Irv Kupcinet strides out again, pats the black comedian on the back. He holds his arms up in a victory sign. Bob Hope is on his way.

A Community Meeting in Uptown: The basement in the People's Church is hot and airless this evening, and jampacked with five hundred residents of the Lawrence Avenue Police District, a poor area on the North side— not so much blacks, in fact, as white Appalachians, American Indians, Spanish-speaking immigrants (with and without visas), Asians, and now one of the newer urban minorities: mental patients, or perhaps outpatients, way-stationed at so-called "halfway houses." Here, too, in a neighborhood of broken glass and broken bricks, is one of Chicago's great centers for day labor—great hiring halls where you show up at five in the morning and get bused off to work somewhere: day wages. The saying is that nobody ever saves enough money this way to buy decent enough clothes to find any other kind of job, but doubtless there are other reasons.

Dr. Preston Bradley, senior pastor of the People's Church and a grand old figure in the city—a white man now in his eighties, his face and speech as familiar to this audience as a child's storybook character—is chairing a meeting whose alleged (and previously publicized) purpose is "to iron out differences between police and citizens in this neighborhood." This evening, Bradley seems especially old and saintly and adroit. "All of us here should be trying to pull together," he intones gravely to the audience, as if it were a congregation. "All of us here should be working to save our community!" Then he introduces a panel of speakers, which includes a Chinese restaurant owner, an administrator from the Hyde Park Jewish Center, another administrator from the American Indian Center, and several blacks, who are described as "citizens."

Police Superintendent Conlisk enters through a side door, surrounded by several policemen, to a burst of applause, particularly from the older white people in the audience. Bradley introduces the Superintendent, and Conlisk now stands before them, and speaks into—or perhaps over—the sea of variously colored faces, softly, almost as if he didn't wish to be heard, and with a strange absence of feeling. His face is very red, and he is sweating a good deal. "Louder!" voices call from the audience, unable to hear him above the milling of the large crowd on the stairs, still trying to get into the hall. The Superintendent appears not to notice the calls. "The record of the Police Department in terms of dealing with the problems of crime and traffic accidents has been a record of improvement," he murmurs. And: "We are making steady progress." Then he introduces First Deputy Superintendent James Rochford. Rochford says that the Chicago Police Department has a "national reputation," and that "people come from all over the world to study our police operations." The large crowd is mainly attentive, but beginning to stir. A row of nine men with the dark faces of Plains Indians sit motionless, staring at the speaker. Rochford says: "The mission of the Police Department is to prevent crime." He says: "The Department has twenty-one districts." And: "Eight thousand men are assigned to them—with over one thousand men on beat patrols." Rochford discusses the "three-minute emergency call." He says: "We have a detective division—one of the finest in the land." He speaks of the "youth division—which we have instituted to work closely with your children so that they will grow up like you." A small argument flares—is quieted—between a group of men who seem to be Mexican, two of them in overalls, no shirts, one with a thin mustache, fierce eyes, an elaborate tattoo along his arm. "Doubtless each of you has experienced contact with our Traffic Division," says Deputy Superintendent Rochford. And: "We are placing increased emphasis on human-relations subjects in recruit training." The hall is hot and becoming hotter. The audience is now restive, murmuring. "We are on your side," says Rochford. "We want your children to feel free." There is a sudden scattered ripple of laughter. Rochford scowls at the audience. "Maybe the laughter is because we have an aggressive Police Department," he says. Then: "You must remember, the enemy is not your Police Department. It is crime and criminals." There is applause, again mostly from the whites.

Now a black Deputy Superintendent, Sam Nolan, steps up to speak about "neighborhood relations sergeants."

There is some jostling and loud voices from the crowd on the stairs. "Crime is a two-way street," says Nolan. "We will leave no limb unturned in our efforts to alleviate the crime situation in our city." A young black man—quite handsome, clean-shaven, not in fact very black, no Afro, perhaps seventeen or eighteen years old—stands by one of the posts in the hall, and next to him there is an older black man, perhaps thirty-five. Nolan is now talking, in a flat instructional voice, about how "neighborhood relations sergeants" are supposed to "work with each district commander as additional liaisons between the police and neighborhood groups and individuals." The young black man says something in a loud voice to his companion. Several heads turn around. Eventually Nolan sits down, and is replaced by a genial, bearded young man from the Jewish Community Center. "You know—to be frank—I sometimes have a hang-up with the police," he says. "I don't always call them up that quickly, and I wonder if this isn't a problem that many of us here share." The young black man and his friend are now talking quite audibly about "murders" and "beatings." Now a black social worker stands at the microphone to say that you "can't always judge a policeman by his uniform." The young black man calls: "Let the *people* speak!" A representative from the Indian center, in a long gown, says that "the situations in our neighborhoods have been ex- aggerated out of all proportion by the media." There is a burst of applause as a large and jivey white man appears beside the stage—the Reverend Hacker, president of the Uptown Community Organization and pastor of the Old Country Church on West Wilson. Much cheering—

Hacker's is a popular voice in the black community. Even the young man and his friend seem attentive. Dr. Bradley introduces Hacker as "that famous television personality from Channel 44." The crowd grows silent. "Now let's hear it!" the young black man says in a low voice. Hacker stands before the microphone. He looks grave. "I want you to think about one thing," he says, "—if we had one thousand bad cops here out of twelve thousand, you know what? We'd have a batting average as good as Jesus—who certainly picked a lemon in Judas." The young black man steps into the aisle. "You're not *black!*" he shouts. "You're not black! How much did they pay you to say that?" The Reverend Hacker appears not to notice, and preaches on about reconciliation and understanding, and about how the police should "try to learn about life on the other side of the tracks." The older black man takes hold of his friend, but then the young man turns and strides out toward the stairs.

After Hacker, another policeman appears: District Commander James Connolly, a large and handsome Irishman. Connolly is there to answer written questions from the audience—a procedure devised to eliminate the shouting matches that had occurred at two previous meetings. The Commander, smiling benignly, opens a slip of paper, and then—in a flat, increasingly incredulous voice—reads: "Why was my kid brother killed by the police?" The Commander is clearly nonplussed by the question, crumples the piece of paper into a ball, and says in an official, nearly inaudible reply, that he "has no knowledge of the incident," but that he is certain "there was no wrongdoing in that, or any other of that sort of case." A

46

voice calls from the rear: "Tell us why they killed his brother!" Connolly stares straight ahead, takes out another question. He reads: "Why do you let these mental patients wander around the neighborhood uncontrolled?" The Commander considers the matter. "Well," he says thoughtfully, "maybe it's true those type of persons don't always button up like they should, and go to the washroom, but basically they are harmless." A young Mexican boy calls: "Hey, who made up the rules for this meeting?" Connolly stands at the microphone. "I invite any of you to visit me in my office, where I will show you my organizational chart," he says. "Oh, I know you mean that!" says a black man. Another voice calls: "Why doesn't he say why the police killed the man's brother?" A number of people are now standing in the hall. Murmurs everywhere. Connolly slips off the platform. There are scattered shouts of: "What about his brother?" The hall is emptying. Up on the platform, the last speaker—Mr. Chin, owner of a Chinese restaurant—takes the microphone. "On behalf of myself and of my family, I want to thank the Chicago Police Department and all its officers for everything they have done for me," says Mr. Chin. The Superintendent has left. The Deputy Superintendents have left. Pastor Bradley and the Reverend Hacker go out by a side door. The audience pushes back down the steps and out into the dark.

QUESTION: Mr. Hanrahan, have you talked to Mayor Daley about this incident?

MR. HANRAHAN: *I* am the State's Attorney and I run the State's Attorney's Office in the manner I believe required by law.

QUESTION: Did you at no time talk with Mayor Daley?

MR. HANRAHAN: *I* am the State's Attorney.

THERE are a number of by-now traditional phrases that people use to try to describe Chicago politics over the past many years. For instance: the city government is run by the Machine, and many or most of the officials have their hands in the till. Or: the city government for the past few generations has been dominated and controlled by the Irish, who operate in league with the Catholic priesthood and with the big contractors and bankers. Or: the city government may be corrupt, but under Mayor Daley at least it "works."

As with most clichés, these are all doubtless true to some degree. Illuminating books have been written about Chicago's corruption, past and present (the most recent of which is Mike Royko's *Boss*), and few of the principal characters have ever stepped forward to raise issues of libel. A recent visitor to the city, in fact, would conclude that the present generation of Chicago politicians could be divided either into those who have been caught finagling in the stock of local race-tracks, or those who have not yet been caught. A while ago, for example, the death of a longtime Secretary of State for Illinois, one Paul Powell, disclosed—within his office—a secret store of shoe boxes containing around $800,000 in cash, most of it allegedly real estate and race-track kickback money. More recently, there has been the trial of Otto Kerner— Kerner, a Democrat and former Governor of the state, was indicted by the Republicans for *his* apparent interest in race-track stocks.

The list of instances of civic corruption in Chicago's history seems nearly endless. Paul Powell and Otto Kerner and God knows whom else today. In the past— well, as every schoolchild here knows, there were the likes of "Bathhouse" John Coughlin and Michael "Hinky Dink" Kenna, aldermen of the notorious First Ward (which contained most of the brothels and saloons) at the beginning of the century, who became patrons of a sort to New York gunman Johnny Torrio, and then to his nephew, Alphonse Capone. And Mayor William Hale "Big Bill" Thompson in the Twenties, who once offered to "punch King George in the snoot," and refused a visit from French Field Marshal Joffre after the war on the grounds that Joffre was "likely to cause trouble," and who also ran one of the tightest Machines (this one a Republican Machine) in the city's long experience with Machines, piled up an enormous deficit, kept Chicago wide open, and was one of the city's first Mayoral builders—he built most of the marinas where the pretty boats are moored. And Mayor Ed Kelly in the Forties, who kept the city wide open and was also a builder—he was in the habit of arranging for the construction of municipal buildings (such as the Cook County courthouse) on land which he already happened to own. And Congressman William Dawson, the powerful black leader of the black wards, who controlled the policy rackets and delivered the Democratic votes that every Democratic President since Roosevelt has needed and sought. And so forth.

Chicagoans still seem fairly prideful of this legendary aspect of their past, and who can blame them? Men were men in those days, whatever that may mean. Heroic figures. Larger than life. Consider "Big Jim" Colosimo, the owner of Colosimo's Cafe, and the man who brought Johnny Torrio and the early Mafia to Chicago (although doubtless they would have come anyway)—"not only did he festoon his person with precious jewels," says an account, "wearing them on several fingers, on his belt, suspender and garter buckles, his tiepin, watch fob, shirt bosom, cuffs and vest, to which he fastened a sunburst the size of a horseshoe, but he also carried about with him chamois bags full of unset diamonds . . ." Who can build a legend around a Commissioner for Urban Relocation?

Corruption, in fact, seems one of the givens in Chicago life, which is obviously not to say that everybody likes it, or is in favor of it, or that people by and large are notably proud of race-track scandals, or of having the profits of their laundries or taverns skimmed by the local syndicate. But Chicago even today, polishing its image, raising tall monuments to clean-living American consumers along the lakefront, is not a place much given to expressions of enormous civic outrage at the escapades of its officials. Officials elsewhere may be just as corrupt, but when, for instance, even in New York a water commissioner gets caught with a paltry $40,000 in his shoe box (as happened a while ago), enough of a row is made—admittedly, an elitist, New York *Times* sort of a row—that (this time anyway) the fellow is packed off to jail.

Lately in Chicago, a Republican U. S. Attorney has been giving trouble to some of the more flagrant Democratic malefactors, but mainly here, one feels, even the elitist minority—or maybe especially the elitist minority—has been inclined to let these things go. From time to time, a reformist or reformlike process will be set in motion, with some initial hubbub in the press, then maybe an inquiry, then maybe a trial, then maybe nothing very much as the original matter is somehow let to come slowly to rest at the bottom of the pond. It is a busy place, people will say. Nobody has time to keep up with all the problems, and issues, and matters of right or wrong, etc. Which is certainly true.

It also seems true that Chicago is one of the last great urban theaters. Indeed, as the clichés say: A number of the politicians do have their hands in the till. And a number of the bankers and publishers and great charity contributors know about it. And nobody ever does much of anything about it because it is all a kind of theater. Everybody has a role. The contractors build their buildings and expressways. The bankers make their loans or whatever it is that bankers make. The politicians feel powerful, dispensing expressway and building contracts. The ordinary citizen rides on the expressways and admires the new buildings. The proletariat receive wonderful patronage jobs, and get to exhilarate themselves with the numbers rackets, and receive advice and friendship from the precinct captains. The city works, because everybody knows what they can do and can't do, and the only thing that can mess it up is if one of the groups of actors decided they don't like the way the play is going—they want not a slightly better role, not a slightly adjusted-upward role, but a different role.

There is also a third category of politician here, as indeed in the rest of the country, a more modern sort of politician (it would seem) who does not have his own hand in the till, or moving toward the till, or even anywhere around the till: which is to say the new noncorrupt politician—the man who himself is deliberately noncorrupt in all the ways that so many politicians have been corrupt, the man who clearly takes no money in bribes, or in real estate kickbacks, or in race-track stock, or in expressway contracts, or in any of the myriad ways that politicians and their lawyers have devised for participating in the national greed.

Mayor Daley seems to fit in this category, and likewise Edward Hanrahan. Neither man, even their detractors say, has taken money on the sly. There may be friends and kin of Richard Daley all over the Cook County payrolls—one of his sons, for instance, works for the insurance firm which handles much of the city's insurance business—but the Mayor himself still lives in his old neighborhood, still lives a modest Chicago-Irish middle-class life, still prefers the company of his old pals, still lifts weights in the morning, and plans a retirement home in neither Palm Beach nor Acapulco, but in County Cork. King Farouk, another sort of leader, lost, or rather mislaid, *his* power-base, but kept a tight grip on his Swiss bank accounts, a nice demonstration of priorities in a man's life. Daley, and his junior associate Hanrahan (who also leads a scrupulously Chicago-Irish middle-class life, with perhaps a bit more noise around the edges), would doubtless have managed it differently.

Daley is seventy years old and an emperor, albeit one whose prestige is sometimes now subject to challenges and discomfiture, and whose power is not as iron-clad as it was. Hanrahan at fifty is a generation younger—a commander of legions, enjoying temporary favor; a Chicago-Irish boy who got himself beyond the usual schools to Notre Dame, and then, on a GI Bill, to Harvard Law School, and then to the attention of Illinois Attorney General William Scott, who made him Special Assistant. Later he became First Assistant. Later, U. S. Attorney. In 1968, Mayor Daley replaced the incumbent in the Cook County State's Attorney's race—an able administrator called John Stamos, who was Greek—with Hanrahan, who was not Greek. Hanrahan won by a wide majority.

"It's his Irishness, you either love him or hate him," is a phrase one often hears about Hanrahan, which seems to mean, when translated, that blacks generally hate him, especially after the Hampton-Clark raid, and many academic and establishment liberal-Democrats appear to hate him (while professing admiration and bureaucratic respect for Mayor Daley, who "gets things done"), and that the still numerous white ethnic groups, many of whom have moved to the suburbs but are still on the Cook County voting rolls, appear to love him. It is all about race, and, as in politics elsewhere in the nation, race is almost never mentioned. "Keep Hanrahan *Your* State's Attorney!" the billboards rather mildly say in 1972. Everybody knows where everybody is.

As to the Irishness, Hanrahan is assuredly Irish, although not Irish in the sense that Jim Farley or Pat O'Brien or even Paul Powell appeared to be Irish—large, garrulous, affable, maybe a bit too sly with the hands, but sweet-talking, full of humors. Hanrahan is neither large nor sweet-talking, being of medium height and medium weight, a man with a pleasant-ordinary face which darkens quickly. His principal physical characteristic, in fact, seems to be his rage, or rather, his capacity for rage. He seems often to be a man on the edge of some inner violence, holding it back. At an ordinary campaign meeting, for instance, standing amid a group of several friends, Hanrahan will abruptly step to one side, arms now folded across his chest, his eyes fixed at some point in the distance, or sometimes at a person across the room—his eyes baleful and glowering. At such times he becomes the only felt presence in the room. Then he will step back into the group, his look lightened, and rejoin the conversation. Had he seen something? Or nothing? It is a strange and powerful attribute: the threat of rage.

"Eddie's very volatile," says a friend. Out at the trial there has been an odd interlude in the courtroom. Barnabas Sears, the elderly Chief Counsel for the prosecution, has protested to the Judge that several times lately he has been harassed by muttered comments from Hanrahan, and that this morning Hanrahan said quietly to him: "I am going to get you when this is over." The defense lawyers say it is a joke. Judge Romiti advises both sides to be more understanding. "Who heard anybody say anything?" says one of Hanrahan's brothers, who attends the trial every day. "Besides, it's just a way of talking."

THE results of the Federal Grand Jury convened under Jerris Leonard in early 1970 had proved oddly unsatisfactory. For one thing, a Grand Jury is usually convened for the purpose of returning either a "true bill" or a "no bill"—in other words, for returning an indictment or rejecting one. This Grand Jury did neither. Instead, in May 1970 it issued a report. The report contained much new evidence, unearthed by the FBI and others, which seemed, at the least, highly questioning of the State's Attorney's version of the raid, and of the subsequent police investigation. The report was also considerably critical of the Black Panther Party, which it described as "violence oriented," "stridently militant," "obsessed with firearms," and "philosophically oriented towards Asian communism"; and of the seven survivors of the raid, who had chosen (under the Fifth Amendment) not to testify before the Grand Jury. Said the report: "The Grand Jury believes that the action [of the survivors] is without legal justification and is nothing more than political posturing to publicize the Panthers' position on juries. Unquestionably, the Grand Jury could obtain a court order requiring the survivors to testify. The enforcement of such an order could thus accord the Panther leaders the martyrdom they seek . . . The time for playing games is over . . . The Grand Jury will not permit itself to be used as an instrument of publicity and recruiting by the Panthers."

The most notable new evidence disclosed in the report was the ballistic evidence. According to FBI experts, who had examined the bullet holes and marks in the Monroe Street apartment, and had inspected and test-fired the police and Panther weapons: *there was physical evidence of between 83 and 99 shots having been fired into the apartment by the raiders, and of only one having been fired by any of the Panthers.* Of the two fired shotgun shells, which had been attributed by the Chicago Police laboratory, at the time of the Special Coroner's Inquest, to Brenda Harris—the "Harris weapon" —the report noted: "At the time of his examination, the firearms examiner from the Police Crime Lab did not have available the weapons the officers had carried on the raid. These weapons were obtained and tested by the FBI . . . the FBI Laboratory positively established that the two shells in question had been fired from Officer

Ciszewiski's weapon (K-25) and had not been fired from the 'Harris' weapon (K-31)."

The Grand Jury report referred to "inconsistencies" in the accounts of the raiding policemen after the raid. It spoke of a police investigation of the event as having been conducted mainly to corroborate the account of the raiders. It quoted the Police Firearms Examiner as saying that he thought his own report had been inadequate (especially since he did not have the police weapons to examine), but that had he refused to sign it he would have lost his job. The Grand Jury found this "alarming," and that the performance of the Police Crime Lab displayed "questionable professionalism." In its strongest criticism of the police, it declared that the performance of the Police Department's investigating unit—the Internal Inspection Division—had been "so seriously deficient that it suggests purposeful malfeasance."

In the end, though, Jerris Leonard's Grand Jury seemed less concerned with the evidence, and with the implications of the evidence, than with the unwillingness of the surviving occupants of the apartment to testify. In the conclusion to its report, the Grand Jury stated: "It is impossible to determine if there is probable cause to believe an individual's civil rights have been violated without the testimony and cooperation of that person." And: "Given the political nature of the Panthers, the Grand Jury is forced to conclude that they are more interested in the issue of police persecution than they are in obtaining justice." And: "Perhaps the short answer is that revolutionary groups simply do not want the legal system to work."

59

Hampton and Clark (whose civil rights, perhaps, had been mainly violated) to be sure were dead. The seven other Panthers (whose indictments for trying to murder the State's Attorney's police had only recently been withdrawn—as a result of the FBI's ballistic evidence) were in hiding, or else locked in their own strange, or not so strange, silences. On page 110 of the Federal Grand Jury's report—the publication of which, it declared in its final paragraph, was "the best service it could render"—had been this observation: "At an absolute minimum, the participating officers say that they were fired at from 3 to 6 times with shotguns, 6 times with pistols, and from 1 to 3 times with unidentified weapons—a total of 10 to 15 shots at a minimum. Only one bullet hole, one shell, and one projectile . . . can be identified ballistically as having been fired by the occupants."

Once again, as a result of outspoken dissatisfaction with the Federal Grand Jury—notably among national civil rights organizations, and certain Chicago legal groups—Judge Joseph Power of the Cook County Criminal Court ordered the convening of another Special Cook County Grand Jury. Barnabas Sears, a well-known Chicago lawyer, was appointed Special Prosecutor. This Grand Jury was assembled in the fall of 1970, and for many months reviewed previous evidence, and also for the first time obtained testimony from some of the Panther survivors. In April 1971, rumors began to appear in the Chicago press that the Grand Jury had voted to indict Edward

Hanrahan and thirteen others connected with the Monroe Street raid. According to the rumors, this Special County Grand Jury had deadlocked 10–10 on returning an indictment for what the State's Attorney's police had done during the raid, but had voted 12–9 to indict Hanrahan and the others for "conspiracy to obstruct justice"—after the raid.

BARNABAS SEARS was sixty-eight years old when he became Special Prosecutor, and is nearly seventy as the trial enters its second month. He is short, stocky, white of hair, with spectacles, and a roundish face—his manner and his speech are somewhat Darrowesque, and he is fond of telling people of his early years as a country trial lawyer downstate in Kane County, Illinois. His later years—most of his career, in fact—have been spent fairly far from Kane County in Chicago, where for some time he has been senior partner in a conservative, or at any rate an establishment law firm, and recently served a term as President of the Illinois Bar Association. His reputation is that of a loner, of a crusty old gent with a strong ego, and a respect for the law. Some years ago, too, when

Chicago was trying to shine things up a bit for its then-new Police Superintendent, the late Orlando Wilson, the police technician from Berkeley, Sears was called in to prosecute a graft scandal against a number of policemen: the so-called "Summerdale scandal." The prosecution was successful. The community—rid of the eight or so pestilential policemen—felt briefly cleansed. Sears enjoyed a period of public acclaim. Some contend that it was a desire to repeat his Summerdale success that compelled him—late in his career—to resume the role of Special Prosecutor, and to pursue his course so doggedly; and there is probably some truth in this: Sears is evidently not without his vanities, and he has made several references during the Hanrahan trial to the golden days of Summerdale. Still, there is more to him than that. He has had a hard time of the Hanrahan case, virtually since it commenced, and with small thanks from anyone (least of all from the Democratic establishment which surely gave him the job in the knowledge that one establishmentarian would rarely go against another), and it has doubtless taken more than vanity to keep him at it.

From the start, he has had troubles with the judge who appointed him—Judge Power, another Irishman, known as a "Daley judge." After the rumors appeared in the press about the Cook County Jury's indictments, Judge Power first told Sears that he had to call more witnesses; then—when Sears replied that this sort of a request to a Grand Jury was not within a judge's province—Judge Power publicly berated Sears; then—when the Grand Jury presented a sealed indictment to Power—the Judge refused to open it, and appointed a director of the Illinois Bureau

63

of Investigation to see if Sears might have acted improperly in obtaining the Grand Jury's vote. In August 1971, four months after the indictment had originally been voted, the problem of at least opening it was resolved by the Illinois Supreme Court, which met secretly in an emergency session and ordered that the indictment be opened and made public.

Judge Power then stepped aside in favor of Judge Romiti, a Democrat who had once been Dean of the Law School at De Paul University. Hanrahan and the thirteen other defendants immediately declined to enter pleas, and instead moved that the indictment be voided—on the grounds that Sears and his assistants had exercised "excessive influence" over the jurors. Romiti ordered a public hearing on the charges of Sears's "improper conduct." Once again, the Illinois Supreme Court stepped in and ruled in favor of Sears. Hanrahan then filed a motion with the United States Supreme Court asking it to review and reverse the Illinois Court's ruling. No payments, meanwhile, had been made to Sears and his staff by the Cook County Board since March—the time of Sears's difficulties with Judge Power. Hanrahan made frequent public attacks on Sears, repeatedly declaring his innocence of any wrongdoing, and saying that it was impossible for a Grand Jury to indict him for obstructing justice, since the event in question—the December 4 raid—had at no time been declared a crime.

At long last, the Illinois Supreme Court refused to reverse its decision. The United States Supreme Court unanimously rejected Hanrahan's appeal, without comment. Hanrahan made one more attempt to derail the proceedings by claiming that the points of indictment put forward by Sears were insufficiently precise, but this objection was also met. Judge Romiti ordered the trial to begin.

A photograph of Sears appeared in the newspapers that summer, at the time of the opening of the trial. It showed Sears smiling, with a homburg at a jaunty angle, and must have been taken several years previously. Now he has the appearance of a much older man.

It is now late July 1972. A hot, slow-moving day in the Cook County courthouse. Deborah Johnson is once again on the witness stand. Thomas Sullivan, lawyer for the State's Attorney's policemen, stands in front of Miss Johnson. He has a thin, paper-covered book in his hand—a children's coloring book published by the Black Panther Party.

"Miss Johnson," Sullivan asks, "isn't it one of the teachings of the Black Panther Party that a pig is a policeman?"

"Not to my knowledge," Deborah Johnson answers.

"Isn't it one of the teachings of the Black Panther Party that all power comes out of the barrel of a gun?"

Deborah Johnson stares straight ahead. It is all a bit like so many discussions on television interview shows, where questions are asked and answers are given, but rarely is the exchange between the actual people on the program—instead the sentences seem to be sent through or past the visible people, and out beyond them to some unseen, soundless, partisan audience.

"Not completely," Deborah Johnson says.

"Isn't it a principle that every member of the Black Panther Party should have a gun and a thousand rounds of ammunition?"

"Not to my knowledge," Deborah Johnson says.

Sullivan begins to ask another question and then stops. It is near the end of the session. "I'll ask you this one tomorrow morning," he says.

But the next day there is confusion and drama in the courtroom. Wayland Cedarquist, one of the assistants on Sears's staff, while examining documents in the office of a lawyer who once represented several of the Panthers, has discovered in a file cabinet certain papers—statements, in fact, which seem to have been made by some of the Panthers shortly after the raid, and which appear to give a slightly different version of their actions during the raid than what they later told to the Grand Jury.

In these new (or old) statements, Louis Truelock says he fired two shots after the police started shooting. Ronald Satchell says he fired once. Brenda Harris says she was holding a shotgun.

Cedarquist gives the statements to Sears, who turns them over to the defense. "It is my duty to protect the rights of the accused in this case, as well as of the people," he says. "We weren't looking for these statements because we didn't know they existed. Now they are here, I have a duty to disclose them." He adds: "First, I have no idea whether these new statements are true or false. Second, in any event they don't appreciably alter the main elements of the case—namely, the disproportionate firepower of the police into the bedrooms, and the covering-up in the subsequent departmental investigations." He also says: "I said at the start I was going to conduct an honest inquiry. Why should I start hiding anything now? To hell with it."

The defense lawyers, however, seem to think that the new statements represent a major breakthrough in their favor. *The Panthers lied!* Sullivan immediately asks the Judge to halt the trial on the grounds of perjured testimony. "CHARGE PERJURY IN INDICTMENT OF HANRAHAN AND 13" says a headline in the *Sun-Times*.

T HE new Panther statements do not cause a stopping of the trial, which Judge Romiti soon orders to continue, but as a result the emphasis in the case seems to have shifted—or perhaps the real emphasis, the location of the real burden-of-proof in the case, has now made itself felt for the first time. It matters not that the police raiders gave out all manner of differing and contradictory accounts in the period right after the raid. It matters not that three supposed new Panther shots were never found, nor that, in any event, they would bring the total of Panther shots to four—four against anywhere from eighty-three to ninety-nine, most of which had been fired by machine gun into the bedrooms. *The Panthers lied* (maybe).

Defense lawyers, who a few days ago had praised Barnabas Sears for making evidence public which might be damaging to his cause, now infer that he had known about the statements all along, and had produced them only when he thought they could be kept hidden no longer. Thomas Sullivan expresses outrage on behalf of his clients (who had arrived at dawn, unexpected, heavily armed, in a time of frequent violent encounters between police and black militants) that the Panthers should have in any way resisted what is always referred to as the "serving of a search warrant," or even have been in a resistant frame of mind. Much is made of the just-found statement by Brenda Harris, a woman, a black woman, that she was holding a shotgun when the police crashed in—as if *this* were the deep offense to the order and safety of society, and in no way to be balanced out by the act of crashing in, nor indeed by the fact that later she had been charged with murder for the firing of two shells which even the police knew she had never fired.

And as for the Panthers—and their silences, and many incivilities, and now contradictions! Had they not entirely been playing Gallant Belgium? "Goddam it anyway," said Wayland Cedarquist during a recess, "the new facts don't make that much of a difference, but if only they could have told us!" Weird Panthers. Had Louis Truelock—the oldest in the group, nearly fifty, already once before in trouble with the law—had he really gone running down that tiny corridor, with the police in back and front shooting all around him, and fired two shots off into somewhere for his own safety, for the sheer *esprit* of it? "Nobody will ever know for sure," says a black journalist, "but I don't think Louis or Ron did any shooting that night. I think they were just the way I'd be—scared to death. I think they were hiding, hiding for their lives. But they were Panthers, weren't they, who were suppposed to be tough and to shoot back at the pigs. It's strange nobody ever found those bullets."

Truelock, Satchell, and Brenda Harris now come to the stand, where they deny or claim not to remember having made the uncovered statements. Francis Andrew also appears—the young, white, activist lawyer who had supposedly transcribed the statements from taped interviews with the Panthers in his apartment two weeks after the raid. Andrews says that he doesn't recall the interviews. "I have only a vague recollection of people sitting around and listening to music," he says on the stand. The court is not amused—Judge Romiti looks alternately fed up and furious. The trial resumes its course, but differently. Both sides now appear to be flawed, and the question is: is there a distinction between the flaws; and who will note it?

The prosecution now attempts to focus on what it considers (at best) questionable procedures followed by the State's Attorney's police, and technicians of the Police Department, after the raid. Earl Holt, a police "evidence technician," admits on the stand that when he arrived at the Monroe Street apartment shortly after the raid he found that the Panther weapons had neither been examined for fingerprints by State's Attorney's police, nor left in place for his unit to examine, but had been removed to a State's Attorney's car, which then took them away. He says that Sergeant Groth, leader of the raiding party, asked him to make photographs of bullet holes in the apartment—holes presumably made by Panther gunfire. "I told Groth I couldn't find any such holes there," Holt says. And: "I said if he could show them to me, I'd photograph them." Holt also says that his superior, Sergeant Koludrovic—one of the fourteen defendants—mistakenly reported bullet holes in one of the bedroom doors as having been caused by firing from the inside, when in fact they had come in from the outside. Some days later, aware of his mistake (Holt says), Koludrovic asked *his* superior, Captain Purtell, if he should change his report. "No. Leave it as it is," said Purtell. Cross-examined the next day by Thomas Sullivan, Holt describes the misstatement in Koludrovic's report as an "honest mistake." He also gives as reason for the careless evidence-gathering procedures that the evidence gatherers "were nervous. It's a very hostile area. It's a high-crime area. We were leery of going near windows and being exposed to snipers."

Still later, Captain Flanagan takes the stand. Flanagan looks remarkably like Superintendent Conlisk—perhaps Conlisk crossed with the late Edmund Wilson: there is that square balding head, the pink cheeks, the solid presence, the massive authority. When asked a question, Captain Flanagan doesn't hem and haw, doesn't pause endlessly, irritatingly, ambiguously thoughtful or hostile, in the manner of the Panther witnesses. Captain Flanagan speaks right out, holding the witness' microphone in one hand, confidently, although sometimes not bothering to use it—his voice, unmicrophoned, amply filling the courtroom with the solidity of his convictions. Flanagan, in fact, presiding from the witness chair, seems at the moment more a judge than Judge Romiti, who appears to have become with each session lately more conversational, informal, disquisitional—a friendly, slightly bored professor, scribbling notes on a yellow pad, trying to stay cool in the late summer heat, and listening to arcane, seemingly disconnected dialogues about police procedures. Flanagan, once of the Traffic Department, more recently chief of the Crime Lab, is addressing himself to a question from defense counsel John Coghlan—himself an Irishman and a former policeman—as to how many of a certain type of illegal shotgun the Crime Lab was experienced in examining in a given year.

"In 1968?" asks Coghlan.

"I'd say about three," says Captain Flanagan without pause.

"And in 1969—prior to December 4?"

"Maybe half a dozen," says Flanagan.

The Captain clearly knows his stuff. Several times he has been described as an expert by Coghlan, who invariably refers to him as "Captain," except when now and then he has preferred to call him "Inspector." Flanagan presently heads the place where John Sadunas worked—Sadunas, the Crime Lab's Firearms Examiner, who had signed his incompletely investigated report, with its references to Brenda Harris' two shots. Flanagan has already attested to the propriety of Sadunas' report. "In my opinion," he said solemnly a few moments ago, "and from my observations, proper procedures were followed at the time."

Coghlan turns away to speak with Sullivan at the lawyers' table. The point of his questions to Flanagan have been to let the Captain affirm his unit's inexperience in dealing with such weapons as the seized Panther shotguns. Once again he faces Flanagan and, as if in puzzlement, asks:

"Captain, sir, would you tell us once more how many of this type of illegal weapon were received for examination by your department in the whole of 1969?"

"One," says the Captain.

Even the Judge looks puzzled. A prosecution assistant makes an objection: "He already said 'three in 1968, and six in 1969 before the raid.'"

Captain Flanagan stares out impassively across the courtroom.

"Let me ask you again, sir," says Coghlan. "How many in 1968?"

"None," says Captain Flanagan.

"And in all of 1969?"

The Captain allows himself a moment's thought. "One," he says. Then adds: "I wasn't listening the first time."

THE late summer heat continues—now Indian summer. The windows of the courtroom stand open but no air seems to come through them. The world outside the courtroom also seems airless, motionless, although scattered, or littered, with reminders of the wild violence of our times. At present: the killing of the Israeli hostages at Munich, and, to be sure, the barely audible newsprint murmurs of the final days of the Indo-China war. There are few visitors in the court these days, and few reporters. Those that come sit placidly with books at their side, or newspapers. On the front page of one there is a picture of a South Vietnamese village after an attack. Or is it a North Vietnamese village? It is hard to tell. One of the last attacks of the war, or so it is said to be. Even as one peers into the wirephoto dots, the scene seems to recede into another cube of time-and-space. Up on the witness stand, Sergeant Fujara, formerly of the Internal Inspections Division, is being examined by Ellis Reid, one of the prosecution staff, a black lawyer—short, compact, with an aggressive walk, and the only wearer of natty clothes in Judge Romiti's courtroom: today a flashy black-lawyer-dude's beige suit, all pockets and lapels.

Fujara, as if by intended contrast, is tall, homely, plain-spoken, and certainly white. In another incarnation one imagines he might make a fine forest ranger—not perhaps the top forest ranger (not at any rate in a remote and fire-prone sector), but anyway a good assistant ranger, all briar pipe and British Army shorts and clipboards, thoughtful, a bit slow, but very steady.

Right now, Sergeant Fujara is with the Juvenile Division of the Police Department. But three years ago, which is by now how long ago it was, he was one of the investigators whom the Police Department assigned to look into the Hampton raid—Sergeant Fujara of the Internal Inspections Division: one of those businesslike, technical-sounding, vaguely threatening titles, which the military and police establishments of modern states like to formulate for themselves; clean modern men, in clean uniforms, just-doing-their-jobs—keeping a sort of sciencelike order among the citizens, and a sort of sciencelike order among themselves.

"Now with regard to Attachment Number Seventeen," says Ellis Reid, himself strangely methodical in his beige suit, "would you please tell us what is Attachment Number Seventeen?"

77

Fujara looks at a clipboard of papers in front of him. "Attachment Number Seventeen is a firearms use report," he says.

"Did you gather that report?" asks Reid.

"Yes, I did," says Fujara.

"Now with regard to Attachment Number Eighteen," says Ellis Reid, "would you please tell us what is Attachment Number Eighteen?"

"Attachment Number Eighteen is also a firearms use report," says Fujara.

"Did you gather that report?"

"Yes, I did."

"Now with regard to Attachment Number Nineteen," says Ellis Reid, "would you please tell us what is Attachment Number Nineteen?"

Fujara furrows his brow and flips through the reports in the clipboard. "Attachment Number Nineteen is an inventory of recovered weapons," he says.

"Did you gather that report?"

"No, I didn't."

"With regard to Attachment Number Twenty," says Ellis Reid, "would you please tell us . . ."

There are roughly seventy of these Attachments on the clipboard—which in sum comprise Fujara's investigation of the raid. Fujara and Reid extend their litany through about thirty more of them. Fujara says "Yes, I did" about some, and "No, I didn't" about most. And then, as if an important point had been made, or else that it has all been far too boring, Reid suddenly stops—walks over to Fujara, retrieves the clipboard, brings it back to the prosecution's table.

The point he has been making, or trying to make, presumably, is that Fujara's report consisted in the main of documents slipped into it by others involved in the raid—but make his point to whom? There is now almost no one in the courtroom except the defendants and the many lawyers. A woman artist for one of the television stations sits listlessly drawing what appears to be the back of the head of one of the defense lawyers. A reporter for one of the afternoon papers—one of the three press representatives in attendance—is flipping through a book on chess. There is no jury. Perhaps the point is made to Judge Romiti. The Judge sits staring off into space, and who can blame him. Fujara continues to sit behind the witness stand—homely, plain-spoken, and blue-uniformed, clearly a man who, were he somehow to make a mistake, would make an honest one. And the clipboard of reports now rests on Sears's table—the reports; the Attachments; the inventory; the results of investigation; the whole paraphernalia of sciencelike evidence.

Commissions . . . Examinations . . . Tests . . . Research . . . Studies . . . Reports: a technocrat, scribe's world of laundry lists—treated nearly everywhere as a kind of truth. Laundry lists about people out of work; about bomb craters in Vietnam; about mothers on welfare; about villages "pacified" in 1968; about the stock market—the fine prospects for airlines or lawn-mowers; about crime—is it up or down? About arson—is it down or up? The congregation sits dutifully in the church. The priest sweeps in. *"Studies show . . ."* the priest intones, and the congregation stands—at that one level, unified.

Ellis Reid has been examining the clipboard of reports,

as if they may yet reveal some secret. Now he gets up again, and brings them back to Fujara. "Your honor, I am once more placing People's Exhibit 55-C before the witness." The reports . . . the laundry lists. Once, they represented the unintentional, or perhaps intentional, mistakes of the men-in-blue: young men, not hugely bright, not very expert, picking up shell-casings here and there, forgetting to do this, omitting to do that, pen and pencil jottings in high-school handwriting, later transcribed by a departmental secretary's typewriter onto the proper forms—careless information transcribed onto the proper forms; and now reincarnated as People's Exhibit 55-C, as Attachments Number Seventeen through Thirty-five, etc. Now, they seem to have a sanctity all their own. One may question—or rather, a lawyer may question—this or that about them; but not what *they* are—what *it* is —to begin with.

Judge Romiti tries to hide a yawn, and nods vaguely at Reid. The hot, airless day is coming to a close. George Cotsurilos, another defense counsel, gets up and asks to look at the reports in front of Fujara. The courtroom now seems mainly to contain lawyers, more or less occupied with Fujara's clipboard. One thinks of the Old Scientism: the clericalism of the Middle Ages, with its endless Synods, Diets, Councils, Bishops, Clerics; men, in fact, seemingly forever entwined with one another, snarled in cobwebs, words, doctrine, meaning, meanings of meaning, and all the while glimpsing less of man, of the world, of the *man* in one another, and certainly less of God—all of them in the end, both wise and foolish, equally trapped by some awesome deference to the Terms of the Discussion.

Cotsurilos now asks to put a question to the witness. Reid stands to one side.

"Sergeant Fujara, would you tell us if you had any difficulty obtaining information from the State's Attorney's Office for your report?" Cotsurilos asks.

"I went over there," says Fujara, "and spoke with them, and they told me to come back in a week."

"But would you describe the atmosphere in the State's Attorney's Office at the time?" Cotsurilos asks. He is a short man, quite dapper in his grey suit; a well-known Chicago trial lawyer.

Fujara starts to answer that he was waiting in one of the outer offices.

"But when you went inside," Cotsurilos asks, "were there not phones ringing, people running about?" Reid objects: leading the witness.

Fujara answers again. He says, yes, the inner office was full of people; yes, telephones were ringing.

"Now, Sergeant," Cotsurilos says—one senses that now he is attempting to make a larger point—"in your three-and-a-half-year experience with the IID, have you ever had an IID file subpoenaed by a defense lawyer in a criminal case?"

There is a chorus of objections from the prosecution. Sergeant Fujara is asked to leave the stand and wait outside. Cotsurilos explains the gist of his question to the Judge. "Your honor, I am attempting to make a simple point. Under the new Discovery Rules, and previously under Moses-Jencks, if statements existed from the police

81

they would have to be made available to defense counsel—"

Sears is now also on his feet. "Who are they investigating anyway?" he asks. "They're supposed to be investigating the police just as much as they're investigating the Panthers. The purpose of an IID investigation is to investigate the facts!"

"The Sergeant had experience in these matters," says Cotsurilos. "He was aware of the law—that this information would have to be made available to the defense."

Sears seems suddenly awake, or more awake than he has been the past while, although his face is white, too white, his shirt is rumpled, his tie askew. "The purpose of an IID investigation is to investigate the facts," he repeats, "and to determine whether any wrongdoing has been done by anybody, including police officers. That's one of the things this case is all about."

"I have one more thing to say," says Cotsurilos.

In the past five minutes, three black men have entered the courtroom and sat down in one of the middle rows. There have been few blacks, now or at any time, in the courtroom, although some appear to be kept waiting outside. Now, one of the men stands up and moves across the aisle—toward the press rows. There is nothing remarkable about his move, except that it is a hot and motionless day, and that his move was sudden, and perhaps that he is black. In seconds, a marshal is at his side. Then another marshal. The black man seems surprised, angry. He goes back to the other men, sits down. Then all of them get up and leave.

"I have one more observation, your honor," says Cotsurilos.

"I think this is a good time for a recess," says Romiti. It is indeed the end of the day. Romiti stands and stretches. Hanrahan leaves quickly through the witness' door. Only some of the police defendants still remain seated, watching the door where the black men had walked so quickly out.

ALTHOUGH Edward Hanrahan is a defendant in a criminal trial, and sits in Judge Romiti's courtroom for most of every day, he is also running for his second term as Cook County's State's Attorney—against a Republican ex-FBI man called Bernard Carey—and thus spends many of his evenings attending small political meetings and giving speeches. A few evenings ago, out in the suburbs (where his political strength is strongest), Hanrahan was talking again about the danger to the community of "street crime," and of the growing threat of the "street gangs" who perpetrate it. "It's a tragedy," he said. "It's probably the worst tragedy we have in our cities. Everybody—black and white, especially the decent people in the black community—are affected by the terror tactics of these gangs. People have told me to cool off about them. I am not going to cool off. It's the biggest fight I have, and I am not going to quit."

Four years ago, when he was then U. S. Attorney for Northern Illinois, and was running for his first term as State's Attorney, Hanrahan said this:

"My concern about crime isn't based on campaign oratory. Rather, it stems from four years of direct confrontation of, and dealing with, criminals of all types; and most terrifying of all—with the true professionals: the career or syndicate criminals. Their lives and those of whom they infect are wholly concentrated on ravaging society, which means you and me and anyone. These men cause a human devastation greater than any I have seen. The State's Attorney, working with our fine Police Department, is in a position to stop this syndicate crime and devastation—can certainly reduce it, and eventually disintegrate it as an organization. I think the most important step a State's Attorney can take is to move energetically and effectively against the professional, organized, syndicate criminal."

Hanrahan's public record as a U. S. Attorney was, in fact, mainly based on his role as a federal crime-buster—and most particularly on his involvement, or on the publicity around his involvement in one case: that of Sam Giancana, one of the top syndicate people in Chicago and in the country. Hanrahan's office sent Giancana to jail for one year—on contempt charges, for refusing to testify when he had been given immunity from prosecution. This was the first time the immunity-from-prosecution device had been used on such a major crime figure. Sam Giancana was in jail, and U. S. Attorney Hanrahan was the man who put him there.

What received less notoriety was when Giancana got out, which he did one year later. Of this moment, Hanrahan has always said that he wanted to reprosecute Giancana but that the Justice Department tied his hands—they were afraid in Washington that if he repeated the immunity process on Giancana at that point, the Supreme Court might throw out the whole device as un-Constitutional. What several of Hanrahan's former assistants say was that the issue was not so much in immunizing Giancana, but in immunizing one John D'Arco, another of the syndicate's top figures in Chicago, who was then, as now, political boss of the First Ward. There was evidence, apparently, that D'Arco and other First Ward officials had made an $18,000 payment to Giancana, and there were those in the Justice Department who wanted Hanrahan to put D'Arco on the stand. What exactly happened then is unclear, except that Hanrahan seemed oddly diffident about proceeding against D'Arco, saying that the evidence was insufficient—and that while the Justice Department and the office of the U. S. Attorney for Northern Illinois were making up their minds on this question, Sam Giancana, who had been out of jail for two days, skipped off to Mexico, where he lives today.

Once in office as State's Attorney, Hanrahan's interest in syndicate crime receded further, or at any rate was displaced by his preoccupation with "street gangs." On the organizational chart which hangs in his First Assistant's office, only two investigators are listed under the heading of "Organized Crime," and the number of indictments pressed against, for example, syndicate gamblers has dwindled from over 200 under the previous State's Attorney (with 130 of them found guilty) to 45 in Hanrahan's midterm (with 33 found guilty), although perhaps more to the point is that, in each instance, Cook County judges saw fit to put only two of the indicted gamblers in jail.

Hanrahan himself has attributed his fairly minuscule activities against syndicate or organized crime to a lack of funds and "not enough staff." But clearly his attentions have been focused on another battle front. "The terror tactics of marauding street gangs," he says repeatedly, "affect far more people than mob crime ever did."

There was a magazine article a while ago, a photo-essay on "Street Gangs": in this instance, a Puerto Rican gang in New York. The text of the story contained the usual sociological earnests about poverty and violence, boredom, frustration—about how life in a street gang is supposed to be an escape from the awfulness of ghetto life but is itself usually even more awful and full of violence. The pictures—many closeups of the sexy-philosophic young gang leader—as often in these matters managed to convey the impression that life in a street gang is really pretty terrific. In any case, very few people seem to *know* about street gangs, or at any rate those who do know seem to be in them, and not outside writing about them.

Street gangs (one gathers) are composed of individual young men, youths (as in "youth gangs"), who appear to be all alike and to act collectively, and sometimes do and don't—as in one of the new Army platoons. Apparently nobody knows too much about the new Army platoons. Recently, a black lawyer in Chicago, Ernest Jones, remarked: "There is absolutely nothing *good* about street gangs," and he may be right. Another black lawyer here, Eugene Pincham, says that the street gang, meaning the black street gang, is the latest in a string of scapegoats that white people keep coming up with in order to account for the real and imagined problems of modern life, and *he* may be right.

It's true in any case that in most of the major cities of the nation there has been increased police proscription of street gangs, which are everywhere mainly black, although in some instances Puerto Rican, or Mexican, or in Chicago also Polish. It's also true that street gangs are responsible for a considerable amount of trouble, mostly in their own communities—a breakdown of the social fabric which strikes many people as appalling, although when we are living at a time when even young, white, reasonably well-paid auto workers have been mucking around at the assembly line, desecrating Henry Ford's Ark of the Covenant, it's hard to see why it should be so surprising that young, black, mostly nonpaid ghetto dwellers are mucking around at their part of the social structure. The point, one imagines, is not whether street gangs are bad or good, or a scapegoat, or a symbol or symptom, but that so very few people seem to wish to try to deal with them at all, with the individual people

88

behind the all-alike black faces—with the men in the platoon.

Now in Chicago there was a brief period in the mid-1960s when there seems to have been an uneven, fragile, not very well organized attempt to somehow redirect the black gangs, to work out some kind of connection between them and what is called the "white community"— a term which still has such a cosy ring to it, a gathering of Vermont villages under a central spire.

Twice, for example, black gang leaders controlled and dissipated near-riot summer incidents on the West side, for which they were duly praised by the establishment and the press. At the time of the Democratic Convention in 1968, when the Chicago police were knocking about at the demonstrators, the black gangs kept their members home and out of trouble, for which they were also praised.

In those days, black gang leaders frequently made public statements to the effect that they should try to stop beating up on one another and instead work together to improve their neighborhoods. An Afro-American Patrol-men's League was founded by black policemen (against the strenuous opposition of the Police Department) to keep an eye on the harassment of blacks by the Chicago police. Saul Alinsky was active in the Woodlawn area. Chicago liberals also appeared on the scene. There was a showing of art by members of a gang called the "Con-servative Vicelords." There was even an attempt somehow to involve members of the largest gang, the Blackstone Rangers, in a musical comedy, and in fact a show called *Black Soul, 1966,* starring several dozen Rangers, was actually produced in a church on the South side, and then a version of it later moved to a theater club on Rush Street where it ran for a short while. But if some whites and blacks at that time thought that the street gangs had a social future, could be a force-for-good-in-the-community, most of the Chicago establishment thought differently, and the city government thought differently, and the police thought very differently.

In 1967, money for a federal antipoverty project was given to the Woodlawn Organization, an offshoot of Alinsky's organizing, which was to be used for "community activities" to be carried out by the selfsame Blackstone Rangers. Not only that—but the federal grant to Woodlawn bypassed all the regular Chicago agencies. The grant—an experiment—was made in fact without city approval, and was for a program to be conducted without city control. In short order, a Congressional investigation of the Woodlawn operation was started, in part at least at the request of Mayor Daley. Chicago police officers testified about "pot and sex parties" that had allegedly been held by the Rangers, and with the knowledge of Woodlawn officials. There were also charges of mismanagement of funds, charges which were more to the point (although precisely to what point?) and indeed which were soon to be heard in connection with the managing of poverty programs in most cities. In due course, the Woodlawn grant was revoked.

One would probably be hard put to show that when the city of Chicago had the Woodlawn grant busted, which is what happened, some significant race-relations landmark was passed. It seems fairly clear at least that the various Robin Hoods among the Blackstone Rangers weren't in any very strong position to run a community program—any more than the Congolese were in a position to run a Belgian electric utility right away, and for the same sort of reasons. And that there was a certain amount of liberal wishfulness in thinking that they could. And a certain amount of rascality on the Rangers' part for saying they would.

What seems to have happened, though, is that the city of Chicago started to take the presence of these street gangs seriously—as a potential social force. And the approach it took to this presence was fairly predictable.

First, the Gang Intelligence Unit of the Police Department was increased. Incidents of confrontation between the police and black gang members also rose—often the same gangs that had helped cool off disaffected black areas in the city during the previous two summers. Black gang members were arrested for putting up activist posters, or for selling activist newspapers. Often young blacks were picked up by police on an alleged violation, or on suspicion of a crime committed somewhere else in the city, and taken to the proverbial vacant lot, beaten, and then left to walk home, or, worse still, left in the territory of a rival gang, with an accompanying phone call from the police that the newcomers were there.

The gangs themselves were not idle. More guns were obtained. Robberies and violence increased in the black neighborhoods. Gang involvement in drugs was also increasing. Shoot-outs between rival gangs which had always been sporadic were now frequent. Even so, some political activity continued. A loose confederation of gangs, called the Black P. Stone Nation, attempted a "No Vote" campaign on the South side to try to take votes away from the Cook County establishment. Later, black gang members formed the majority of demonstrators who closed down the city's construction industry for several weeks, demanding more jobs for blacks in the building trades. And in November of 1968, the Illinois Chapter of the Black Panther Party was chartered by Fred Hampton, a young black activist from nearby Maywood, a leader of community and high-school protests, who had recently spent close to a year in prison for allegedly having stolen 210 ice-cream bars from a Good Humor Truck.

Then, in the spring of 1968, Mayor Daley and his new State's Attorney Hanrahan announced their "War on Gangs." It was a formal, well-publicized event. The Mayor summoned his more important officials to plan "strategy" for the war. The Superintendent of Schools, the Fire Commissioner, the Police Superintendent, and, with the usual ironies of bureaucratic nomenclature, the Commissioner of Human Resources were named to a top-level "planning board." State's Attorney Hanrahan, who had formed an elite nine-man squad, the Special Prosecutions Unit, to deal with street gangs, took public leadership of the war.

"Without question, the Black Panther Party represents the greatest threat to the internal security of the country."

—*J. Edgar Hoover, Director of the FBI, 1968*

"We consider the Panther organization probably the most dangerous in the nation."

—*Chicago Police Department, 1968*

"I'm sure that Mr. Sears would like to see us veer away from the Black Panther philosophy, but the central question in this trial is the attitude and propensities of these people. Our policemen didn't go out there in the predawn hours to serve a search warrant on the Altar and Rosary Society. They went there to serve warrants on people who for years had been issuing threats to kill, and even printing coloring books showing children how to kill police."

—*Thomas Sullivan, defense counsel, 1972*

IT IS hard now to remember the way that much of white society regarded the Black Panthers when they first appeared in the late 1960s—those fearsome, frightening, arms-bearing black men, with their paratroop berets, and swagger, and revolutionary rhetoric. The first student uprisings, Mario Savio and the Berkeley "Free Speech" movement, and the first antiwar protests had not come that long before—our kids, our nice kids, lying down in front of troop trains, using profanity in public, trying to upset the establishments of universities. And now: black men with guns.

On May 2, 1967, in the course of a debate on a new gun-control measure in the California legislature in Sacramento, twenty-six Black Panthers marched into the

State Assembly, openly (and legally) carrying shotguns, rifles, and pistols—to demonstrate, they said, their opposition to the new proposals. There was pandemonium in the Assembly. State senators scurried under desks, or ran to take cover. The Panthers stood in place, and then let the security guards take the weapons and unload them. The Panthers pointed out that no charges could be brought against them under the current law because the weapons were not concealed. When the unloaded guns were returned, the Panthers, wearing their black leather jackets and berets, marched out again, and drove back to Oakland.

Oakland was where the Panthers started. Oakland—which now has those flashy athletic teams on TV, but not so long ago was better known for being one of the toughest cities in the country, full of slums and out-of-work blacks, and with a tough police force and William Knowland's *Tribune* to help keep things in line. At first, there was a small group of young black radicals at a local city college—who admired Stokely Carmichael and Malcolm X, and some of whom had read Frantz Fanon's *The Wretched of the Earth*—and who called themselves the Soul Students Advisory Council. Out of this later came a smaller group called the Black Panther Party for Self-Defense.

"We have chosen the panther as our symbol," said Huey Newton, one of the founders, "because it is not in the panther's nature to strike first. But when he is backed into a corner he will respond viciously and wipe out the aggressor." The Panthers were strong on rhetoric. They published a ten-point program, much of it in a kind of

Maoist jargon, calling for decent housing, full employment, black juries for black defendants, an end to "robbery by white racist businessmen," an end to police brutality. "We want decent education for our black people in our communities," said Point No. 5, "that teaches us the true nature of this decadent racist society, and that teaches black people and our young black brothers and sisters their rightful place in this society." Blacks should control their own status and values, said the Panthers, without "dependence on, or exploitation by, the white establishment." If necessary, force should be used to achieve this.

It was a time when even blacks, who so recently had been coloreds or Negroes, were themselves barely getting used to being called black. It was a time of much strident talk, especially from what was then called the Radical Left, about racism, and fascism, oppression, and the white establishment. The Panthers were determined to be a model to young blacks—especially young black men. They bought guns. At first, they scrupulously observed the various gun laws, and risked public confrontations with the Oakland police so as to show other young blacks that it could be done—if a white man can carry a gun legally in public, this symbol of manhood, why not a black man? They dropped the "Self-Defense" from their name, and became the Black Panther Party.

Force. Guns. Political programs. It never worked very well. For one thing: too many guns. For another: too many macho-conscious, angry young blacks, some already with police records, others not yet with police records but aware that in their country, at that period, the fact of being a Black Panther was all the certification one would ever need. The Panthers bought uniforms at Army surplus stores, and shined their boots. They practiced military drill. Adventurous TV cameramen would show us pictures on the evening news of a Panther squad practicing close-order march. They were strong on military discipline—after all, didn't the establishments of all great nations have this in common: a high regard for uniforms? And tried to be strong on other disciplines as well, proscribing alcohol and drugs, doubtless in many instances a losing battle, but also in many instances not. Strange black outlaws, living in the same ghettos they had always lived in, but now dressed as soldiers—dressed, in fact, in the manner of President Kennedy's Special Forces bravos, and raging against the police, the pigs, the whites, all the while stirring pots of stew, scurrying around after fifth-hand Spanish carbines, mimeographing barely intelligible pamphlets, shining their beautiful terrifying boots; and trying (surrounded by the drug decadence which is perhaps the only thing that white suburbs and black ghettos have in common) for their own weird purity—a modern outlaw's purity.

It is difficult to remember much of this, or much of that special mixture of fear and fascination and hatred with which so many whites (as well as blacks) regarded these Panthers, because for a while now things have been quite different. The specific of protest, of anger, in this country, which at one point seemed about to grow into a larger wave, never somehow grew; somehow receded, or became engulfed again into the mainstream. Mick

97

Jagger, perhaps, remains our only public radical. And as for the Panthers—most of them seem to have been killed, or are dead anyway, or in jail, or disappeared; receded or engulfed, maybe, into some other dimmer mainstream. And one remembers: there were never so very many of them to begin with.

Our country, in fact, has a way of loosing its fears and angers on some remarkably thin-ranked adversaries: Senator Joseph McCarthy's "Communist conspirators" of the 1950s, the radical-leftist students of the 1960s, and the Black Panthers, who in their heyday (such as it was) never numbered—at least, according to FBI estimates—more than six or seven hundred members scattered around the country. Doubtless not a group to be ignored, but, even so, a force slightly smaller than a battalion of National Guard, should it ever have assembled one morning (borne together by Greyhound bus and hitchhiking) on the plains at Yorktown.

In Illinois in early 1969, again according to the FBI (which certainly used to keep check on such things), the Panthers had between thirty and forty members, with probably twenty-five to thirty of them in Chicago. The whites were angry and afraid of them. A majority of blacks were angry and afraid of them. Who wants more trouble? Who wants another gang? Who wants a lot of talk about "capitalist oppression," and still more guns in the neighborhood?

There was this difference, though, between the Panthers here and the other gangs: which is that the Panthers, for all their guns, and tough talk, and acts of toughness, were serious, or trying to be, about black pride, and black control of their communities, about "liberating" blacks from official and police harassment, and also about proscribing alcohol and drugs (the ghetto vices), especially drugs. Whereas by this time most of the black street gangs had moved further and further away from any thoughts of social programs, and closer and closer, in spirit and in operations, to the traditional gangster-modeled gangs of previous years. There was a rising amount of intra-ghetto violence, of "street crime." There was also (as there is today) a steady increase in extortion and drug trading—in other words in the classic areas of mob capitalism.

By the spring of 1969 (the same spring when the "War on Gangs" was declared), the Chicago Panthers had begun moving into several new areas—not new in terms of the Panthers, who had begun similar ventures in Oakland and San Francisco, but in terms of the Chicago street gangs. One was in the area of social action, specifically a well-publicized, although small program of "free breakfasts" for poor ghetto kids, and a beginning attempt at "free medicine" for needy black families.

Many whites, especially in the city government and police, said that this was only a front—that the Panthers were as murderous and antisocial as ever, and had only gone into the free breakfast and medicine business in order to dissemble what they were really up to. It's certainly true that Panthers were forever trying to amass guns, and that their rhetoric was as steamy as always; although the evidence seems to be that—with the exception of several instances of "sniper fire," which the police invariably claimed came from Panther headquarters, coincidentally when police squad cars were in the vicinity, and which were invariably later disputed by the Panthers, as well as by street witnesses—the Chicago Panthers had never gone on an armed rampage, had never tried to storm police precincts, or take over radio stations, or even hold up merchandise vans, the last-named activity being then, as now, a favorite of the ordinary gangs.

The other area that the Panthers were venturing into was in trying to unify the other gangs, the street gangs—to politicize them—and it was in this area that Fred Hampton had appeared most visible. By then, police harassment of all the black gangs, but especially of the Panthers, was very strong. An official of the Chicago Police's Gang Intelligence Unit testified before a Senate Committee on subversive activity that the Chicago Panthers had lately gone in for the "soft sell"—and were embarked on a program of forming coalitions with other gangs. In May 1969 a press conference was called by Fred Hampton of the Panthers, by representatives of the Blackstone Rangers and of the Black Disciples (traditional rivals of the Rangers) to announce a truce between the gangs. "Now we are all one army," Fred Hampton said.

By the end of May in Chicago there had been ninety-five arrests of Panthers. On June 4, 1969, forty FBI agents raided Panther headquarters on West Madison Street, ostensibly looking for one George Sams, who was not a Panther but was wanted for murder of a Panther in Connecticut. Sams wasn't there, but the FBI said there was evidence of his having been there, and arrested the eight Panthers present for harboring a wanted criminal. Later, the eight were released. The Panthers also charged the agents with confiscating money from a cashbox, and destroying food supplies for the breakfast program. The FBI denied this.

Four days later, Chicago police stopped a car full of Panthers near Panther headquarters—for traffic violations —and charged the occupants with possession of explosives and narcotics. These charges were later dropped.

On June 19, a Panther, David Smith, was arrested for selling the Panther newspaper.

On July 3, Bobby Rush was arrested for a traffic violation and released on $300 bail.

On July 8, a Panther, Willie Calvin, was arrested for selling the Panther newspaper.

On July 16, two Panthers, Grady Moore and Larry Roberson, were involved in a shoot-out with two policemen. The two policemen were wounded. Both Panthers were charged with attempted murder. Roberson later died from wounds received in the shoot-out, and the charges against Moore were dropped.

On July 30, a Panther, Lockett Bibbs, was arrested for a traffic violation. On the same day, five Panthers were arrested for possession of marijuana. Both charges were later dropped.

On July 31, five policemen and three Panthers were wounded in a gunfight near Panther headquarters. Police said they had been fired upon from the Panther offices while on routine patrol. Panthers and street witnesses said the police had fired first and had then tried to set fire to the offices. Panthers claimed that more food supplies had been destroyed. Charges against the three Panthers were later dropped.

Another incident took place on October 4. Once again, police said they had been sniped at while on patrol near Panther headquarters. Panthers said there had been no snipers and that the police had fired first. Six Panthers were arrested and charged with attempted murder, with bail set at $100,000. Panthers claimed that afterward police had poured gasoline on their office and set it afire. Charges against the six Panthers were later dropped.

Still another incident took place on November 13: a gunfight between Panthers and the police, which eventually involved fifty policemen, and resulted in the death of one Panther, Spurgeon Winters, and of two policemen, Officers Gilhooly and Rappaport. The death of Gilhooly, whose father and grandfather had been senior Chicago police officers, was especially noted in the press.

The Chicago press indeed (as did the national press) seemed mightily interested in the Panthers during this period. Between December 1968 and December 1969, Chicago newspapers printed well over two hundred articles about the Panthers—the speeches of their leaders, their gunfights with police, their theories of Communism, their proposed mergers with street gangs, etc. On one hundred and thirty days of that year there was a piece about the Panthers in one of the main Chicago papers— or on one out of three days of the year.

Nor was the State's Attorney's Office silent about the "War on Gangs." A Special County Grand Jury had been empaneled to consider indictments against gang leaders, and Hanrahan's office almost daily announced an account of returned indictments, which by the fall of 1969 totaled over two hundred. Hanrahan himself made countless speeches and radio broadcasts, in many of which he described gang members as "vicious animals," or "animals unfit for society." He expanded his elite nine-man Special Prosecutions Unit to eighteen men.

There is a photograph of Fred Hampton taken around that time, in the fall of 1969. He is standing on a Chicago sidewalk, presumably making a speech. Dr. Spock is off to the right, eyes half-closed, perhaps from the sun or else from the rhetoric. Hampton's mouth is open in the photograph. He wears a dark cap, dark shirt, a kind of leather jacket. He has a roundish face, young—and long dark sideburns. Behind him, barely visible, is the building where the Panthers had their headquarters. *A headquarters!* Thirty to forty men in all of Illinois. A shambly set of offices in a shambly part of town. Old brick and peeling plaster. Full of wild posters and rhetoric and bits of paper and too much coffee and very little money and some food supplies and those guns. Never without the guns—although even with the guns it was never much like General Patton's headquarters. Still, a headquarters is what they called it, and so we called it one too. These mostly young black men (it sometimes seems) had this one fantasy, which was not unfortunately of playing corner back for Pittsburgh, or even of being vice-president of Xerox, but instead a dreamlike mishmash of Founding Father radicalism, Marxist rhetoric, and Western-sheriff-paratrooper manhood. And we, seated in

103

our well-locked apartments, our carefully zoned villas, listening to the unclear new sounds out on the street, perhaps mesmerized by the strange shine on those boots —in the end we wrapped this fantasy around their necks.

T HE air is cool now, cool and wet—no Indian summer any more. For days the sky has hung low over the city. People walk about in overcoats and raincoats, walking warily toward winter. Fall now. The baseball season is nearly ended, with the White Sox finally out of the running, a fact much discussed, lamented, then finally comprehended on the multitudinous sports pages of the city newspapers. There has not been much interest by the press lately in the Hanrahan trial. A few reporters come in and out of the courtroom, sit for a while, scribble snatches of testimony on the backs of envelopes. The reporters say their editors are bored by the story. Recently, it has mostly been a matter of hearing more witnesses who were connected to the Police Department's investigation of the raid. Today, there is a rumor that Police Superintendent Conlisk will appear as a witness for the prosecution, clearly a prosecution coup—but it turns out this is not so, not today at any rate. For one thing, a cheerful, earnest, slow-speaking Sergeant of the Investigations Unit is continuing his testimony. For another thing, Senator George McGovern is in town on his curious campaign, and Edward Hanrahan absents himself for a couple of hours to take part in the official ceremonies.

The event in question, in fact, is billed in the press as a "reunion" or "reconciliation" between McGovern and Mayor Daley, and is attended by no less a personage than Senator Ted Kennedy, the current Grand Duke of the Democratic Party, whose entourage has descended on the city in the early morning—a ducal private jet whooshing into rainswept O'Hare, duly received by Mayoral representatives, and then transported by fleets of police cars (the expressway suitably blocked to other traffic) toward the Mayor, and the Senator from South Dakota, who had arrived earlier.

The historic meeting is held, neither on the Field of the Cloth of Gold, nor even on a private railroad car parked in a forest, but (perhaps appropriate to the times) at the Sherman House, a businessman's hotel across the street from City Hall, in the Louis XVI Suite, which is a large and loony chamber full of mirrors and pink cherubs on the walls. It has become a filthy, rainy day, and not a morning one would normally pick for public spectacles, but Mayor Daley, he of the Old Politics, who only two months ago was being hassled by

McGovern's staff for seats at the Convention, has magically arranged for the nearby streets to be roped off, for large numbers of citizens to stand in the rain behind the ropes—and for the flower of Cook County politics (certainly of Cook County Democratic politics, which is usually the same thing) to array itself beneath the cherubim of the Louis XVI Suite, there to receive the pilgriming McGovern and the gallant Grand Duke.

The Mayor begins the speeches by announcing, or at least saying, that Senator McGovern will be "our next great Democratic President," a matter he does not dwell on. He then describes the campaign as being "unusual and peculiar." And then, in grand and ringing tones—a bit like a cheery Norman king, imperfectly versed in English, leading a bunch of Saxons into battle—he declares: "And we will win in November if only we will get out and articulate this campaign!"

The next three speakers—Cook County elegances Pucinski and Rostenkowski and candidate-for-Governor Daniel Walker—each repeat the wondrous phrase: "We will win in November if only we will articulate the campaign!"

State's Attorney Hanrahan appears to have no special keenness for articulating the campaign. When Daley introduces Dan Walker, Hanrahan does not applaud. He and Walker have a feud, largely as a result of Walker's refusal to endorse Hanrahan. Walker himself is a middle-aged liberal lawyer who has been campaigning around the state, giving off boyish charm and a kind of unctuous Populism, which he mainly expresses in this gathering by furrowing his brow a lot, and trying to appear at once purposeful and detached in the presence of so many Machine stalwarts. Now he concludes his speech, which has been full of references to "social issues" and to "bringing the issues before the people," by saying, in the apparently expected manner of all New Politicians, that he hopes soon "to be working in Springfield for a better Illinois as our own great Mayor Daley has been working for a better Chicago."

Mayor Daley then stands to introduce Hanrahan. "And now I introduce to you a great fighter," says the Mayor, transforming himself from Norman king to prizefight announcer, "and our next State's Attorney—Edward V. Hanrahan!" There is applause, rolls of applause. People stand on chairs in the back of the Louis XVI Suite, clapping and cheering. The next day even the New York *Times* remarks on it. "By far the largest applause was for incumbent State's Attorney, Edward V. Hanrahan," says the *Times*, which then went on to dutifully observe that "Mayor Daley needs the office of State's Attorney in the Democratic fold," and, more to the point, that Hanrahan was running only one or two points ahead of his Republican challenger, Bernard Carey, in the polls.

Hanrahan now stands, expresses a few combative phrases about how nobody there "has anything to feel defeatist about," about how *he* certainly didn't, and that there was going to be a big victory in November—and sits down. Suddenly Cecil Partee jumps up—a black man, President pro tem of the Illinois Senate, one of the Mayor's black men. "I just want to say that we need Ed Hanrahan in office to give us the kind of peaceful community that I like to live in!" says Cecil Partee. More standing and cheering.

Then Kennedy and McGovern speak. Kennedy draws a big hand, but you have a feeling that the people here are still a bit cool on him, that they think he let the side down in Miami—here, after all, was the Golden Boy, the Golden Boy they had helped *make* as a politician, and when they needed him he had gone waffling off to Cape Cod, drifting around on a boat off Hyannis while Daley and Tom Keane and the real Democrats were getting kicked in the head by the longhair, computer-printout bastards on McGovern's staff; drifting and waffling and giving out statements about "family duty" or "responsibilities in the Senate," while the Grand Old Machine found itself nearly dismantled in the hot Miami sun, left in a heap on the dock, then hauled (grudgingly) aboard the Good Ship McGovern, she of the creaks and leaks and underpowered engines and no fuel and poor dining facilities, and now were being asked for God's sake to save this same crew and this same weird ship.

"We have the issues and the candidates!" intoned the Grand Duke. "The question is, whether the Democratic organizations will do the work they have done so well in the past!" Presumably, stuffing ballots. "Will you do the *work?*" inquired the Grand Duke, tall and tan and terrific beneath the cherubim. "Will you knock on doors? Will you ring doorbells? Will you do for the Party in 1972 what you did in 1960?"

Kennedy sits down amid applause—good applause for anyone else, but not remarkable for a Kennedy—and with vague (vaguely troubling, vaguely exciting) emotions about the departed JFK now floating around in the Louis XVI Suite.

Then McGovern. His Scots brow seems clear and resolute—he seems very much the only Scotsman in that assemblage. One wonders what he feels about this particular meeting? Is it a Canossa (do Scotsmen go to Canossa)? Or is it an act of Reunifying the Party? Had there ever been an Old Politics and a New Politics, and had there ever been a difference between the two, and did the difference matter? Mayor Daley stares benignly ahead. Pucinski and Rostenkowski keep their eyes on Daley. Hanrahan glowers briefly at no one in particular, and looks at the floor. Dan Walker, as usual, seems to be trying to look like Lincoln.

McGovern says that Daley is "the great Mayor of a great city." He says that Daley "has proved that a city can be made to work." He says: "The Democratic Party I worked to build in South Dakota is the same Party, and works in the same way, as the Party that Mayor Daley heads here in Illinois." He says: "I intend to work for the entire Democratic ticket from top to bottom." The Mayor smiles, a tiny smile on a large hard face. McGovern for Pucinski. McGovern for Cecil Partee. McGovern for Hanrahan, our fighting State's Attorney. "Would McGovern support Ted Kennedy in '76?" The question is not asked, although it is asked of Ed Hanrahan if he will support Dan Walker in 1972. "I'm running for State's Attorney," says Hanrahan.

Afterward, Mayor Daley asks McGovern, Kennedy, and all the Cook County merrie men to step outside the Sherman House, where they can be rained upon and receive cheering from the crowd. Only Hanrahan declines, heading out a side door to a waiting car, which will return him to the courthouse. Outside the Sherman House, George McGovern, the nominee of the Democratic Party for President in 1972, is standing beneath an umbrella and saying: "I say here that I would trade the support of John Connally and his Wall Street friends for the support of State Street." Ted Kennedy, not standing beneath an umbrella (did Rose bring up those boys to stand beneath umbrellas?), says: "We are going to come from behind and win in 1972." There is applause. Pictures are taken of the faces of the important men on the sidewalk in front of the Sherman House. And everybody goes home.

THE best way to get to the Cook County courthouse from downtown is like this: first, get out of the downtown—the ancient stodgy Loop, with its overhead tracks, and old-fashioned shops, and adult movies, and beer & brew restaurants, and black movies, and occasional wondrous new insurance company highrises—and head west, away from the lake, and the huge tall visible skyscrapers, away from the Sears tower and west along the Eisenhower expressway, which was once the Congress Street expressway, and before that Congress Street. The Eisenhower runs seemingly off toward the horizon. The tall buildings fall away. To the left there is the Chicago Circle campus—another Chicago architectural triumph: a cluster of elegant, fortresslike buildings in a sea of shops and boardinghouses. Ashland Avenue. Paulina Avenue. To the left again: Cook County Hospital. They took the wounded Panthers here, and many many others. At Cook County Hospital, emergency cases are treated in order of entrance rather than in order of emergency—a system of logic, which (it is said) produces some unusual scenes. Cook County Hospital, it is said—periodically in the press and by Republican candidates—is "too political." Now we go further west—the traffic thinning out—past Western Avenue; then California Avenue and off the Eisenhower, off the comfortable wide grey asphalt with its passenger traffic and trucks of recognized manufacturers, and suddenly into neighborhoods. *Neighborhoods. Don't tear down the old neighborhood.* One imagines it must depend a lot on who is doing the talking. This neighborhood is Lawndale, an area of Chicago which is usually referred to by people who live elsewhere in that helpless and vaguely condescending tone ordinarily reserved for small African countries. Here is the great Southwest side of Chicago. Here is Laura's Lounge and the Horizon Rooming House. Here, too, is the Douglas Park Church of the Brethren. Also: the Twenty-fifth Ward headquarters (Vito Marzullo, Committeeman). Also the Industrial Skill Center, and the Latinos Travel Agency. (What tours, one wonders, depart from the Latinos Travel Agency?) The brick is everywhere dark and dirty brown. A group of six black men in their twenties and thirties sit and stand upon the porch of a boardinghouse. The men mostly have jackets on, and some wear hats, and one has a beer, and appear to be motionless, silent. There is Rita's Pool Hall. Also a laundry. Then: the Cook County Criminal Court building: a massive cube of masonry; a spot of lawn in front; a flagpole; police squad cars parked at the curb. Behind the courthouse, mostly hidden from sight, is a nearly twin building: the Cook County Jail—even as prisons go, a much disliked place, although it is mainly a way station for men awaiting trial.

On the courthouse lawn today, spread out in rows, are the two or three dozen paintings of a Prison Art Show. The paintings are mostly scenes of action: football and boxing. Also: two women making love on an American flag; a picture of prisoners struggling in chains; and a flattering portrait of Jacqueline Onassis. Above the stone steps, seals of the city and the county, as well as some mythic bulls and eagles, and chiseled promises of "Veritas" and "Justiciae" somberly decorate the outside of the grey granite edifice—surely if there were ever an "edifice," this is it. One already feels a bit punished for having looked at it. Inside, most of the clients seem black; as do the Sheriff's aides, who stand on either side of the doors. There is a search for weapons: manly pats on the jacket and on the seat of the pants. A powerful-looking black policewoman attends the ladies, who are in a long line and chattering.

In Judge Romiti's courtroom, the atmosphere becomes less shabby and more reassuring. After all, here is Edward V. Hanrahan on trial, clearly a respectable and not a shabby person—not the sort of person for whom there are armed Sheriff's aides to search jackets and pat trousers—now surrounded by lawyers and other police persons, also a brother and two bodyguards (certainly not a deviant or a regrettable person among them), all of them holding their own in these proceedings against "Veritas" and "Justiciae." And there is Barnabas Sears, distinguished lawyer, his head resting against the back of his chair. There is Judge Philip Romiti, wearing an orange shirt beneath his robes, cocking his head in his hands—a bit pensive, a bit irritable. If murder were ever to be discussed in this courtroom, one would expect it to be a more reputable sort of crime than the wretched activities that are evidently discussed in the other courtrooms of this building. In Judge Romiti's courtroom there are no descriptions of stabbings and gore, no anguished recollections or pleas; instead the clear cool droning of professional witnesses, and the theatrically controlled voices of the lawyers.

The courtroom today is more crowded than it has been lately. More press, and several blacks. Today the last Investigations Sergeant departed, and the court awaits Superintendent Conlisk. There is an air of tension and expectancy in the courtroom. Conlisk's word carries much weight in certain parts of this city. He is the Police Superintendent—the Mayor's Police Superintendent.

In fact, back on December 11, 1969, it was Superintendent Conlisk who first ordered the Internal Inspections Division to investigate the Hampton raid. The investigation promptly stopped—for procedural reasons: a question of jurisdiction over the State's Attorney's police. It was a request from Hanrahan that got it started again. Conlisk then directed Deputy Superintendent Mulchrone to conduct "a complete, comprehensive investigation of the facts." Mulchrone passed the word down to Captain Harry Ervanian, who was then Director of the IID. Ervanian immediately announced that "all information relating to the raid" would be examined, including "arrest records from the raid, all physical evidence, statements from the witnesses, and photographs of the apartment."

On December 19, 1969, Captain Ervanian then issued his celebrated report:

"Physical evidence," he wrote, "has fairly established that the occupants of the premises fired upon the officers who were in the process of executing a search warrant. There is no apparent misconduct or impropriety by any of the officers . . . the officers were in the process of lawful execution . . . they were met with deadly force . . . the officers were obligated and lawfully justified in countering this deadly force . . . this investigation is classified as exonerated and recommended that no complaint register number be issued."

Some months after this, the Federal Grand Jury subpoenaed Ervanian's files, which had been kept private, and discovered that in fact they contained "no records of contact with neighborhood residents; no indication of a visit to the premises; no ballistic analysis of the officers' weapons compared to the recovered bullets and empty shells; and no detailed or substantive account of the incident by the fourteen individual officers, although the latter appeared for questioning on December 16, 1969."

This "questioning" of the officers had been under the nominal direction of Deputy Superintendent Mulchrone, who in turn had selected Sergeant John Meade, a former Assistant State's Attorney, to "advise" him in the matter. Sergeant Meade revived his knowledge of the incident by watching a tape of the State's Attorney's television "re-enactment." Then he put together a list of questions to be asked of the raiding policemen.

Later, the Grand Jury asked him:

Question: Would it be fair to say that in drawing up your questions, you took the version of the officers as being the truth?

Answer: That is correct.

Question: Were there any questions on your list that tended to test the truth and veracity of these officers?

Answer: No. I assumed that everything they said was true.

Meade then discussed the questions and answers with Mulchrone, and three Assistant State's Attorneys, and Sergeant Groth, who at the time was the leader of the men who were being investigated. Groth then was allowed to examine and alter some of the questions and answers. When the thirteen other policemen arrived for the "questioning," the three Assistant State's Attorneys took them aside and briefed them on the questions; and then Sergeant Meade and Sergeant Groth went through the questions and answers, with Groth assenting to the answers, and the thirteen policemen assenting to Groth.

Thus did the Chicago Police Department investigate the Monroe Street raid.

Some time later, while testifying before the Federal Grand Jury to the effect that neither he nor anyone in his office had "received any pressure" from anyone in the Police Department, Captain Ervanian of the IID admitted that the investigation had not been developed "with any great degree of accuracy." A juror asked:

Question: Do you consider this a normal investigation?

Ervanian: No, sir, this was not a normal or complete investigation.

Question: Captain, let's be candid: now, with the State's Attorney's Office represented at this meeting, and the man who led this raid, or the service of this warrant, and the way the questions were drafted, and the ultimate questions which were asked of these officers—Captain, do you think it would be in any way unfair for a reasonable person to conclude that this was nothing but a whitewash?

Ervanian: The way you describe it, no, sir.

Question: Again, Captain, even adding the facts of the Crime Lab report, would it be unfair or unreasonable for a person to conclude that this was a whitewash?

Ervanian: I would agree, sir, that this was a very bad investigation, yes, sir.

Question: Well, it was extremely bad, wasn't it?

Ervanian: Yes, sir.

Question: As a matter of fact, have you seen one as bad as this one?

Ervanian: No, sir.

When Superintendent Conlisk had come before the same Grand Jury, he had said that he was "aware that the questions to be asked the officers might have been discussed with the Assistant State's Attorneys." When informed that the proposed answers had also been prepared and discussed with the Assistant State's Attorneys and Sergeant Groth, the Superintendent had replied: "I am flabbergasted to think that such a thing could exist."

And now we are two years later, and the Superintendent is once more being asked about the Monroe Street raid. He seems large in the witness stand: appropriately grave; a bit diffident. A General of Troops. Sears is patient, almost courtly.

"Superintendent, tell us when did you first hear about the incident?"

Conlisk: I heard about it on the morning of December 4. I understood we were involved in investigating it.

Sears: And what did you do?

Conlisk: I called Deputy Superintendent John Mulchrone and ordered that the investigation be terminated.

Sears: Did you have any further discussion about the investigation?

Conlisk: Yes, about three or four days later I received a call from Mr. Hanrahan. He said he felt it was important for us to continue the investigation.

Conlisk then speaks of summoning Mulchrone, of reordering the investigation, and of a conference with Mulchrone on December 19, when Mulchrone had declared that "all avenues had been pursued to the fullest extent possible," and Conlisk had then issued a press statement saying that the investigation was complete.

Sears: But were you aware on December 19, 1969, that questions prepared and showed to investigators had not been used? Were you aware that the IID had not concluded its visit to the premises at 2337 West Monroe? Were you aware that no check had been made of neighborhood people, of hospital personnel who handled the wounded—

John Coghlan, a defense lawyer, runs nearly shouting toward the bench: "Objection! Objection! Mr. Sears is leading the witness!"

Sears also seems to be angry. "I am not leading the witness," he replies, "because I am not suggesting the answers." He returns to Conlisk.

Sears: Now, Superintendent, when did you become aware of these facts? Was it at a conference in my office?

Conlisk: Yes.

Sears: And how many meetings did we have on this subject?

Conlisk: Three.

Sears then turns to one side for a moment, looking past the defendants and their lawyers, pauses, turns back to Conlisk.

"Superintendent," he says, "now, in the light of these matters that have come to your attention, do you have an opinion at this time as to whether it was a complete and thorough investigation?"

The courtroom is quite still. It is the key question.

Conlisk looks straight at Sears. "I do. At this time, I think it was a complete and thorough investigation."

The defense lawyers are openly jubilant. Sears is silent —his head in fact is lowered. There is much noise in the courtroom. Sears raises his head. "Superintendent, but you testified on February 23, before the Grand Jury, that you did *not* think it was a thorough investigation—" There is too much noise in the courtroom, and Conlisk is excused. Later he returns. He explains that a "report on the incident" made by Sergeant Groth had been "added to the earlier report," and that that had made the investigation complete. Groth's report, the Superintendent says, "detailed the police version," and "it all checked out."

Sears asks: "But wasn't it last Thursday that we spoke and you told me you still felt the investigation was incomplete?"

Conlisk: Yes.

Sears: Have you talked to any of the defense attorneys since last Thursday?

Conlisk: Yes, I spoke to John Coghlan.

Sears: And did you and John Coghlan discuss the Groth statement?

Conlisk: Yes, we did.

Sears seems about to ask another question, but then stops. He looks at Conlisk. Conlisk stares impassively ahead. "I have no further questions," says Sears. The Superintendent—the prosecution's star witness—rises, and is led out of the room.

A COLD, wet, windy morning. The press is full of accounts of the bombing of the French embassy in Hanoi—the inadvertent bombing by one of our airplanes. There are pictures of wounded French diplomats. Pictures of rubble. The story is played very big, both in the papers and on television news. The Nixon administration at first denies responsibility, and talks vaguely of a North Vietnamese antiaircraft rocket having gone awry. The press —apparently suddenly stunned to moral fervor by diplomaticide—prints lengthy expressions of outrage from foreign capitals, and a few editorials of its own on the "random destructiveness" of bombing. It is a curious business—not so much the event, which must surely have occurred sooner or later (and probably has), but our quickened response to it. It is as if, for the first time in months or in years, the war has come alive: as if the gratuitous terribleness of the war (which we have known all along was there, hidden in the communique jargon of "strikes" and "missions" and "raids") were briefly made visible; and not through the face of a Vietnamese, of whom we have seen so many—men, women, and infants, numberless, faceless—but through the stretcher-borne French consul. The French consul dead! White faces in the rubble!

It is a flat, dull day at the courthouse. Robert Zimmers, a retired FBI ballistic expert, is on the stand. He is a short, trim man—pink of face, close-cropped hair, strangely old and strangely youthful in appearance: a Western face. He speaks in the classic manner of FBI witnesses—professionally; his testimony full of names and dates and numbers, especially numbers, and delivered in the manner of a technician trying to be reasonable— a busy technician, who would prefer to be back at his post, but is willing to appear before us briefly and give much-needed technological coherence (as well as dignity) to what would otherwise be the shambles of hearsay, and approximation, and well-meaning laymen.

Inside the courtroom, the rows of visitors are nearly empty. The defendants are present—visibly bored. Officer Davis, a tall, lean black man with a reputation for meanness, sits in a chair beneath one of the windows, and makes imitation-trombone music with his hands. Officer

Corbett passes a note to Sergeant Sadunas. There is virtually no press, except for two women artists (drawing their per diem from TV stations) and a man from the *Sun-Times*, and a young boy from one of the wire services, who is reading a book.

Wayland Cedarquist, an assistant prosecutor, is leading Zimmers through what appears to be an endless series of questions about ballistics.

Cedarquist: Would you please describe item Q-4?

Zimmers: Q-4 was one of the items I recovered myself in connection with a search of the apartment on 2337 West Monroe Street. Upon examination, they were shown to be .00 shot pellets.

Cedarquist: Would you please describe item Q-11?

Zimmers: Q-11 was the bullet I removed from the south wall of the north bedroom. It is a .30 carbine bullet.

Cedarquist: Would you please describe item Q-14?

Zimmers: Q-14 is a bullet that was removed from the north wall of the south bedroom. It is a .45 automatic weapon type of bullet. It was fired from the Thompson submachine gun.

Cedarquist: With regard to Q-14, who recovered that?

Zimmers: It was recovered in the course of a search of the premises at 2337 West Monroe Street.

Cedarquist: Would you please describe item Q-28 . . .

Over to the right side of the courtroom, a few feet to the right of where Barnabas Sears is sitting (his face once again pale white, his head thrown back against the chair, his clothes rumpled) is the grey wood mock-up of the Monroe Street apartment. In his flat professional voice, Zimmers continues to enumerate the "items" that he and his staff (working then for the Federal Grand Jury) picked out of the walls, or in some cases off the floor, or out of a pile of clothes in the Monroe Street apartment. Part of the purpose of this exercise, presumably, is to show the court the number of ballistic items that had not been picked up by the State's Attorney's men or the regular police. In fact, the State's Attorney's men picked up sixty or so items; the Panthers' lawyers subsequently found forty-three more; and some weeks later the FBI team found another thirty. Presumably, it is a point worth making, although the court seems mesmerized in boredom. Judge Romiti hides a yawn behind a hand, and writes another note—about Q-28? about lunch?—on his yellow pad. Officer Corbett writes another note, and passes it down the table to Sergeant Groth, who reads it and smiles.

In this courtroom today, it is hard to remember that there was a raid. There were, we know, "ballistic items." There was an "investigation." There is even the grey wood mock-up in the courtroom, with the metal dowels criss-crossing the bedrooms, indicating the trajectories of the incoming bullets. Zimmers drones on about "recovered shell fragments" and "test firings," and Cedarquist, the prosecutor—apparently tied to Zimmers in this litany, two priests chanting in an empty church—leads him further into this strange cube of time: not the time of the raid (for there was a real raid), nor even this morning's time (for this is a real morning; our soft mortal bodies sit on the wood benches of the courtroom following their own distinct trajectories), but some kind of legal time, a semi-time, a metaphor of time.

Question: Would you please describe Q-29?

Answer: Q-29 is a caliber .380 cartridge, unfired.

Question: Are there any markings?

Answer: There are none.

Question: Would you please describe item Q-241?

Answer: Item Q-241 is a jacket—that is, a steel jacket from a .30 carbine bullet . . .

It's hard to know exactly what happened in the course of the Monroe Street raid because so many conflicting accounts came out of it, and each side—true to its own logic, and history, and private code—has done either a small amount, or a large amount, of lying.

"We tried our best to avoid loss of life or wounding anyone. I called on our men to stop shooting, and they did. I asked the other people to surrender, shouting that we had a search warrant, and they didn't obey . . ." The metal dowels in the mock-up, and the austere semi-scientific testimony of Zimmers, are about all that remains in evidence—acceptable to our world—that Groth's version was wrong. Even so, for all that it was a real moment bloodied with violence and killing, Groth's view of it (his

statement was made one day after the raid) seems almost touching—perhaps at once touching and ghastly, in the manner of soldiers who use the mythology that we once taught them to describe (i.e., reorder for their sanity) the frightfulness of war.

It is a familiar scenario, after all. The band of gallant men. Not wanting trouble, not looking for a fight—just adoing of their duty. The Boys in Blue. The Thin Red Line. Jeb Stuart's cavalry. Lord Kitchener's patrol. Shots ring out! A fusillade from hidden crannies, from behind bushes! The calm voice of the young leader rises above the din. "Men! Stop shooting!" The men, sweat-stained from the desert sun, their faces blackened with powder smoke, lay down their guns, stand at the ready—the older, smarter ones pause to reload, keep an eye out for furtive movements in the bushes, for betel-stained faces against the rocks. The young officer advances across the plain . . . the veldt . . . the sagebrush. "Ho, there, fellows!" he calls. He waves a search warrant in his hand. "I bring a message from the King, or perhaps the President, or anyway General Allenby. He sends blessings on your dreadful heathen heads and says you should open your door, or perhaps your ravine, or country—" Suddenly a spear lands at his feet. Fierce, awful-looking tribal bowmen appear on the battlements. "Curses on your President Allenby!" call angry voices in various dialects. "We will shoot it out!" The young officer walks back to his gun emplacements. Already, the men are loading up the big Navy ten-pounders. "All right, men," he says—there is a trace of sadness in his voice—"return fire." Spears and arrows thud harmlessly into the ground. The

Navy ten-pounders roar. "Do what you have to," the young officer says, "but, for God's sake, no more."

Thus the West was won—or was it India? Or MGM? We have killed most of the Indian Nation, and many Mexicans, and many Cubans, and many Filipinos, and, of course, the grandparents and parents of many Volkswagen and Fiat employees, to say nothing of nearly vaporizing the port which sends us Sony television sets; and in each case, it seems, a young officer has said: "Men! Hold your fire!" and an angry heathen has snapped: "Shoot it out!" In Vietnam, it is true, the young officer has not been so visible, the grizzled veterans have not shaken their fists so often, nor rode into battle swilling Castilian wine—although, perhaps when it really counted, when we wanted a description, another reordering for our sanity, the young officer reappeared. "You never knew who was friend or foe at Mylai," he said. "The children sometimes lay in ambush. The women all had guns."

"Our men had no choice but to return fire," said Sergeant Groth. He is a pleasant-looking man in his thirties —dark hair, a bit heavy in the face. He wears a grey business suit, white shirt, conservative tie—he might be an accountant, or a partner in a small business.

In the early morning hours of December 4, 1969— around 4 A.M.—thirteen Chicago police officers, presently attached to the State's Attorney's Special Prosecutions Unit (dealing mainly with black gangs), met, under prior arrangement, with the leader of the group, Sergeant

Daniel Groth, in the State's Attorney's Office in downtown Chicago.

The formal steps that had occurred up to then were these:

On November 21 an FBI informant had passed on a report that the Black Panthers had a cache of weapons and ammunition at 2337 West Monroe Street. The FBI listed the weapons, which appeared to show no violation of federal gun laws, and the seven Panthers who were most frequently seen at the apartment, and forwarded the report to the Chicago police and to the State's Attorney's Office.

On November 23 the FBI found out that the Panthers had removed the weapons from the apartment (expecting a police raid on the twenty-fifth) and called the police —who confirmed that a raid had been planned, and would now be canceled.

Then, on December 1, the FBI learned that the weapons had been returned to the apartment by the Panthers, and passed this information along again to the police and the State's Attorney, again listing the weapons, which appeared to be legal, and legally purchased, and the principal occupants, including Hampton, Satchell, Truelock, and Deborah Johnson.

Finally, on December 2, Sergeant Groth received private information that among the Panther weapons at 2337 West Monroe Street were three sawed-off shotguns, and three stolen Police Department shotguns. Groth immediately told Richard Jalovec about this—Jalovec then being the Assistant State's Attorney in charge of the Special Prosecutions Unit. Jalovec told Groth that he too had received similar information from the FBI as to the presence of illegal weapons in the Panther apartment, and the presence of Fred Hampton—apparently Jalovec here had confused the FBI's report of three Ithaca "riot shotguns" (which were not illegal), with Groth's report of three sawed-off shotguns, which were.

On the afternoon of December 3, Jalovec prepared a complaint for a search warrant. "A reliable informant," says the complaint, ". . . informed the affiant, Daniel Groth, that on December 2, 1969, he had occasion to enter the above-described premises at 2337 West Monroe, first floor apartment. During this visit, he observed numerous weapons, including three sawed-off shotguns . . ." Sergeant Groth then signed the complaint before Judge Robert Collins, and advised the men on the Special Prosecutions Unit to draw suitable weapons, and to meet at four that morning.

The fourteen policemen assembled on schedule. Hanrahan was not present, nor was Jalovec, who said later that he had met with Hanrahan around five on the previous afternoon, when he told him that "State's Attorney's policemen would be serving a warrant for Panther weapons in the morning." Jalovec told the Federal Grand Jury that he considered the raid "a normal thing," and probably wouldn't have informed Hanrahan of it if he hadn't been discussing "other matters" with him at the time.

Groth briefed his men—who should come in by the

front, who by the back. All the policemen were in plain clothes. As weapons they had brought: one Thompson submachine gun (with 110 rounds of ammunition); three police shotguns; two privately owned shotguns; one privately owned carbine; nineteen .38 caliber pistols; one .357 caliber pistol. They had with them no teargas; no portable sound equipment, such as a bullhorn or megaphone; no lighting equipment. Around four-thirty the fourteen men left the State's Attorney's Office in three unmarked police cars, and a paneled State's Attorney's truck, and headed out toward West Monroe Street.

A normal thing. Chicago, December 1969: already a cold winter. Nearly each day more arrests are announced in the "War on Gangs." In the new Federal building, the "Conspiracy 7" trial unfolds in Judge Hoffman's courtroom. Each day, Jerry Rubin and Abbie Hoffman, the two white media-revolutionaries, offend the Law with their antics. Panther Bobby Seale, the only black in the group, as if to show that Panthers must do more than prance and taunt, one afternoon is physically held down by marshals, and gagged, and bound, and carried from the courtroom. Not much more than two weeks ago has been the police-Panther gun battle, in which patrolmen Gilhooly and Rappaport (and Panther Spurgeon Winters) were killed.

Now: fourteen policemen in plain clothes, armed with twenty-seven firearms, including five shotguns, a carbine, and a submachine gun, are driving west at four-thirty in the morning to present a search warrant.

T HE RAID: It takes no more than fifteen minutes to drive, at dawn, from downtown to West Monroe Street. At about four-forty, Sergeant Groth, who was in the unmarked lead patrol car, radioed the then-nearby Thirteenth District police station to send two more patrol cars to cover the front and back of 2337 West Monroe. This was the first notice that the Chicago police received about the raid. A few minutes later, Groth and his men arrived at Monroe Street near the Panther apartment. They parked the three cars and truck a few hundred feet south of the apartment, and went toward it on foot.

Sergeant Groth climbed the few stairs to the front porch, accompanied by Officers Jones, Hughes, Gorman, and Davis. Officers Carmody, Ciszewiski, Broderick,

Kelly, Joseph, and Corbett went around to the back. Officers Marusich, Harris, and Howard remained outside to cover the front and rear of the building.

The time was about four forty-five in the morning. Groth had a .38 caliber revolver. Jones had a .38 caliber revolver and his own 12-gauge, double-barreled shotgun. Gorman had a .357 caliber revolver, and a .45 Thompson submachine gun. Davis had a .38 caliber revolver, and his own .30 caliber carbine. The four men stood (they said) within the entrance foyer. Groth (he said) knocked at the door to the apartment.

Within eight minutes, the shooting was over. At about 4:54 A.M., patrol car no. 1101 from the Thirteenth District, which had arrived on the scene with several other police patrol cars, reported by radio that "the premises were under control." Hampton and Clark were dead, and their bodies were taken to the morgue. Of the surviving Panthers, Blair Anderson was wounded twice, Verlina Brewer was wounded twice, Ronald Satchell was wounded five times, Brenda Harris was wounded twice —and were taken to the Cook County Hospital. The remaining three Panthers were taken to jail. Officers Ciszewiski, who had received a pellet wound in his leg (fired through a bedroom wall, presumably by one of the other officers), and Carmody, who had cut his hand on some glass, were treated at the University of Illinois Hospital that morning and released.

And what had actually happened? "There must have been six or seven of them firing," said Sergeant Groth, the morning after the raid. "If two hundred shots were exchanged, that would have been nothing," said Officer

Carmody. And Groth again: "Shotgun fire kept coming at us from a room off the living room—the room behind where the girl first opened fire on us." Ciszewiski said: "We fought our way from room to room. I don't see how we got out with only light wounds." Richard Jalovec issued a statement to *Chicago Today:* "Sergeant Groth and Officers Ciszewiski and Carmody went to the back door, where Sergeant Groth announced: 'Police, police, we have a search warrant.' Male and female voices from within the apartment called out 'Who? Who?' This exchange continued for several minutes." Sergeant Groth informed *Chicago Today:* "I knocked at the front door and someone asked 'Who's there?' I identified myself as a police officer and said I had a warrant to search the premises. I received no response. I repeatedly demanded entry for several minutes."

Officer Ciszewiski said: "As soon as we announced that we were State's Attorney's police, a burst of shotgun fire came though the back door." State's Attorney Hanrahan issued his statement: "The immediate violent criminal reaction of the occupants in shooting at announced police officers emphasizes the extreme viciousness of the Black Panther Party. So does their refusal to cease firing at the police officers when urged to do so several times." Jalovec issued another statement: Officers Davis and Jones had gone to the front door where they were "seeking peaceful entry by proclaiming their identity and the fact that they had search warrants . . . Davis heard shuffling or scuffling inside, followed almost instantly by blasts of gunfire." Groth said to the *Sun-Times:* "When I heard no response from any of the occupants, I put my shoulder to the front outer door and forced it open." In the *Tribune*, Groth said: "I heard a male voice call out, 'Who's there?' I replied: 'This is the police. I have a warrant to search the premises.' . . . 'Just a minute,' a male voice replied. Suspicious of the delay, I ordered Officer Davis to kick the door down."

The first-floor apartment at 2337 West Monroe Street consists of a living room, two bedrooms, a bathroom, dining room, and kitchen. The apartment is small: the distance from the front to the back door (i.e., from the living room to the kitchen) is less than forty feet. At four forty-five on that morning, no lights were on.

Davis said: he crashed into the front room. A shotgun blast went past him—from Mark Clark's gun (the only Panther shot recovered). He said that Brenda Harris fired two shotgun blasts. Groth fired his revolver. Davis fired his carbine, killing Clark, and wounding Harris. Carmody—arriving through the back—said he saw several gun flashes and "a hand holding a gun." Carmody fired in the direction of the gun flashes. Broderick, behind Carmody, fired a shotgun blast into one of the bedroom walls. In the front, Gorman, with his submachine gun, and Davis, with his carbine, fired toward the back—but into and through the wall of the front bedroom. Jones, also in the living room, heard firing from the back—from the back bedroom, he said—and fired his shotgun into the front bedroom wall. In the back, Broderick saw "two shotgun blasts light up the front bedroom," and fired two shotgun blasts of his own into the back bedroom. In this period of time, Gorman was firing a full magazine of thirty rounds with his submachine gun into (and through) the front bedroom wall; Davis, with his carbine on automatic, was firing about a dozen rounds. In the process, Sergeant Groth said he called several times for a cease-fire. Panthers Bell, Truelock, and Deborah Johnson had surrendered. Clark was dead. Brenda Harris wounded. Fred Hampton was found dead in the back bedroom. In the same period, Ciszewiski called that he had been shot. Broderick, still in the back, said he saw "flashes from the front." He ran toward the front, and then fired several shotgun blasts into the back bedroom. Gorman meanwhile had reloaded the Thompson submachine gun with another thirty-round clip and moved toward the front bedroom. Said Gorman: "I slammed through that doorway, firing a burst into an open closet I spotted out of the corner of my eye. I saw two beds with the forms of two people rising between them. One had what looked like a shotgun. As he started to aim, I fired, and the gun fell as he did. The second form kept rising, and I fired again after I saw something that looked like a handgun in the person's hand." By the time Gorman had finished in the small bedroom, he had emptied his thirty-round clip. Carmody followed Gorman into the room with his revolver, but did not use it. Panthers Anderson, Satchell, and Verlina Brewer surrendered.

The Federal Grand Jury estimated that between 83 and 99 shots were fired by the State's Attorney's police that morning. According to the FBI examination: seven were fired from revolvers; between 12 and 25 were fired from

12-gauge shotguns; 19 were fired from a carbine; and between 44 and 48 fired from a Thompson submachine gun. The one shot recovered from a Panther weapon was the single shell from Mark Clark's shotgun.

THE death of Fred Hampton: On the morning after the raid, the State's Attorney held a press conference. Said Mr. Hanrahan: "This morning, pursuant to a search warrant, State's Attorney's police attempted to search the apartment at 2337 West Monroe Street and seized sawed-off shotguns and other illegal weapons stored there. This disgusting display (on the table in front of him) shows how effective the search was by our officers . . . I point also to the automatic revolver which was used by Fred Hampton in the course of the attack on the police when they were carrying out the search warrant authorized by the court . . ."

The back bedroom at 2337 West Monroe is proportionately as small as the rest of the apartment: a room about ten feet by eight feet. On the night of the raid, it contained a double bed (taking up about half of the room), a small table, a chair, and a reading lamp. On that night, two people were asleep on the bed: Hampton and his girl, Deborah Johnson, who was then nineteen, and nearly nine months pregnant with Hampton's child.

Said Deborah Johnson of that evening: "I arrived at the apartment soon after midnight. Fred and Louis Truelock were talking about something in the living room. We spoke, then I went into the back bedroom, then I returned to the living room and spoke some more with Fred, and then I went back to the bedroom and went to bed. Fred got into bed about one o'clock and we phoned his mother and sister and spoke about thirty or forty minutes." In the course of the phone call, Hampton fell asleep. "After I got off the phone, I tried to wake him, but I couldn't," she said. Then Deborah Johnson went to sleep.

The next thing she said that she remembered was Louis Truelock, the eldest of the nine Panthers, shaking Hampton on the bed beside her, trying to wake him. "Chairman, chairman! Wake up! The pigs are vamping!" Truelock was saying. By then, she said, the darkened apartment was lit with gunfire. Hampton still had not stirred. "I heard what sounded like gunshots. It was so many I couldn't count them," she said. "I looked up and I saw what appeared to be—it looked like shooting was coming from the front of the apartment to my right, and also from the back, the kitchen area." Truelock was partly on the bed, next to the still-dormant Hampton. Deborah Johnson crouched over him. "I looked up again and there seemed like about a million pigs converging on the door of that bedroom," she said. She started to move Hampton's body toward the edge of the bed farthest from the door—where she said that police were now firing into the room "so that the mattress was vibrating real fast from the bullets being shot into it." She was now lying partially over Hampton. "I looked at him. I saw no blood on his face or on the bed. Then, Fred raised his head up and looked toward the door. He didn't make a sound. That was the only movement he made, and then he laid his head back down, and I laid my own head down because I thought I was dead and that was it."

Truelock, meanwhile, had moved off the bed and was crouching by the wall. He kept yelling: "Stop shooting, stop shooting! We have a pregnant sister in here!" She said: "Truelock was shouting, and all the while there were all these police in the doorway." The shooting continued, she said, and Truelock kept shouting: "Stop shooting, stop shooting!" Then the shooting stopped.

She said: "Truelock called 'We're coming out.' I put my house shoes on. I had my hands up. Truelock was coming out behind me. Then I heard two single shots. I couldn't see where they came from. I jumped, keeping my hands up."

Outside the bedroom, she said she saw two lines of police. "One of the policemen grabbed my robe and threw it down and said, 'What do you know, we have a broad here.' Another man grabbed me by the head and shoved me into the kitchen." While standing in the kitchen, she said: "I heard a voice from another part of the apartment saying: 'He's barely alive,' or, 'He'll barely make it.' Then I heard more shots. A sister screamed from the front. Then the shooting stopped. I heard someone say: 'He's as good as dead now.'"

The FBI determined that a total of twenty-six rounds of ammunition were fired into the back bedroom—most of them machine gun bullets which were fired through the walls from the living room, and shotgun blasts which were fired from the doorway. Hampton was shot four times: twice, mortally, in the head; once in the left shoulder; and once (a graze) on the right arm.

The first autopsy was performed, early on the morning of December 4, by an assistant pathologist at Cook County Hospital. Somehow the assistant pathologist's notes on the autopsy were lost or destroyed, but by then they had been incorporated into a "pathological report" by the acting director of the hospital. This report said that (in addition to the shoulder and arm wounds) Hampton had been shot twice in the head. One shot (said the report) went in on the left side of the head, and went out the right; the other went in at the right of the neck, and went out the left.

Two days later, at the request of Hampton's family, another autopsy was performed by a Dr. Levine, former Chief Pathologist at Cook County Hospital. Dr. Levine was assisted by four doctors and a lawyer. He said that Hampton had been shot twice in the head, but that both shots had traveled from right to left. The crucial bullet, said Levine, had entered the right side of the forehead and passed through the brain. "The track of this shot," he said, "was probed to a point behind the left eye, where no exit wound was found." There now seemed to be a missing bullet. Dr. Levine suggested that perhaps the coroner might have found and removed one from behind Hampton's left eye.

A third autopsy was held—doubtless a fairly grisly affair—this time in Shreveport, Louisiana, where Hampton's family came from and where he was buried, and was attended by Dr. Charles Petty, Chief Medical Examiner of Dallas County, Texas; Assistant Attorney General Jerris Leonard; representatives of the Cook County State's Attorney's Office; two FBI agents; four Deputy U. S. Marshals, and a half-dozen lawyers.

Dr. Petty found that both previous autopsy reports had been in error. It was true, he said, that Hampton had been shot twice in the head—both shots traveling from right to left: one shot through the neck, the other entering at the right forehead. But this second and crucial shot, he said, instead of terminating mysteriously by the left eye, could be seen to have exited "from a wound in front of the left ear, which was clearly visible when the sideburn covering it had been shaved away."

Dr. Petty's report (which was made for the Federal Grand Jury in 1970) contained one other item of interest. After Hampton's death—because of statements by Deborah Johnson and Louis Truelock that they had been unable to wake him—there had been allegations to the effect that perhaps Hampton had been drugged, had been given a heavy dose of sleeping powder, possibly by the same informant who had sufficient access to the apartment to tip off the FBI.

The Cook County Coroner's Office immediately denied the rumor, and said that Hampton's stomach had been opened during the first autopsy, and nothing unusual had been discovered. Item 4 of Dr. Petty's report merely stated: "Contrary to previous reports, the stomach had not been examined. The stomach was found to be attached and unopened." So much perhaps for the Science of Pathology, as well as for Resting in Peace.

In the end the Federal Grand Jury "accepted" Dr. Petty's overall report, and chided the Cook County Coroner's Office for its errors, which it chose to attribute to "understaffing" on the Coroner's staff. As to the interest in which side of Fred Hampton's head the two fatal bullets entered, it is probably this: if the two bullets had come in from different sides, the probability is that Hampton was active, or at any rate moving; if, as it turned out, both bullets came in at the same side, within a few inches of each other, then the probability is that either Hampton was motionless, or was shot at very close range, or both.

One more finding at the time of the third autopsy was as follows: "Paraffin tests performed upon the body of Fred Hampton were completely negative, indicating that he had not fired a weapon of any sort immediately before his death."

BUT it is 1972 now, and Robert Zimmers is still on the stand. Already he has testified for several days, and it is expected he will continue for several days more. The courtroom is nearly empty. There is a mist outside, and a light rain blows against the windows.

On the floor of the courtroom, below Judge Romiti, there is a large mattress, which has been dragged into the room by two Sheriff's aides, and arranged on the floor by Wayland Cedarquist, the assistant prosecutor. The color of the mattress is pink or beige—it is hard to tell because the thing is old and dirty. There are holes on the side and on the front, and places where the mattress covering has been cut off and pieces of the stuffing exposed.

One whole corner of the mattress—more like a quarter—is stained with a brownish substance, as if someone long ago had once spilled chocolate on it.

Nobody in the courtroom looks at the mattress—even the one remaining lady television artist who seems to be determinedly sketching Judge Romiti for the one hundred and eleventh time. The Judge looks in the general direction of Zimmers. Zimmers looks at Cedarquist. Sears has his head back and seems again to be staring at the ceiling, perhaps dreaming of the good old days in Kane County, or possibly of Oliver Wendell Holmes, whom lately he has been fond of quoting—perversely twanging the great Justice's nineteenth-century *pensées* into the politburo stonework of the Cook County courthouse. The defendants seem to be looking nowhere, as they have for most of Zimmers' arcane, methodical enumeration of the bits of shell and cartridge and casing and shot and pellet that he had examined from the apartment they had visited so long ago.

Now, Cedarquist asks: And did you recover item 162-I from this mattress?

Zimmers: Yes, I did.

Cedarquist: Would you please describe that item?

Zimmers: The item consisted of three small fragments of lead.

Cedarquist: Did you observe any additional holes in the mattress?

Zimmers: Yes, I did. There was one large hole on the top surface of the mattress. There was a hole near the center. There were several holes near the center . . .

One of the defendants, Officer Gorman, stands up and closes the window behind him. Corbett passes a note to Ciszewiski, who passes it on to Davis. Zimmers' voice is flat and dry and untiring: an astronaut's voice, perhaps, to go with his retired-astronaut's face—the simple declarative technocrat sentences plopping back on us from some invisible far-off experience, although in this instance, in this courtroom, there appears to be no journey under way, no point of departure, no expectation of ultimate arrival anywhere.

Fred Hampton's mattress lies on the floor. It seems a naked, shabby thing, although possibly even new mattresses seem naked, and all old mattresses seem shabby. This one has a brown stain covering the top quarter of it. Mr. Cedarquist and Mr. Zimmers discuss the matter of holes.

Cedarquist: Would you tell us please if there were any holes at the label end of the mattress?

Zimmers: Yes, there were.

Cedarquist: And did you remove anything from these holes?

Zimmers: Yes, there were three fragments removed from these holes.

Cedarquist: Now, were there any holes at the end of the mattress opposite the label end—on the end or at the sides?

Zimmers: I have no such holes charted . . .

One is aware that this ballistic catechism has been heard before: first, two years ago by the Federal Grand Jury; second, one year ago by Sears's County Grand Jury, and the matter at issue now is not the *event,* but whether the fourteen defendants "obstructed justice" as to the aftermath of the event. The defendants' lawyers seem indifferent to Zimmers, except when now and then one of them will rise to question, or anyway to briefly jostle Zimmers' flat expertise. "You say you made a scientific examination?" one will ask. "With what equipment did you make that examination?" Zimmers replies: "In that instance, with my eyes. I have made sixty thousand such examinations . . ."

Cedarquist continues: Now, I would like to ask you about the holes on the east end of the mattress. Did you examine those holes?

Zimmers: Yes, I did.

Cedarquist: Well, do you have an opinion as to whether the holes on the east end of the mattress have a relation to the holes in the east wall?

Zimmers: Yes, I do. There is a definite relationship between the holes on the east end of the mattress and the holes in the east wall . . .

The rain continues to fall on the windows. Somebody goes for coffee. Two black men come in and sit down near the back, and then get up again and leave. The mattress lies between Cedarquist and Zimmers—a liberal white lawyer and a dutiful white technocrat. It seems a curious place for Hampton's mattress to have ended, although in fact it mainly resides in a county warehouse— also an unlikely place. Now, two black girls and an older man sit at the back. The marshals briefly turn to look at them, to check them over, then glance away. One wonders what the marshals see. Three people? Two girls and a man? Three faces? One doctor and two Indian chiefs? Three candlestick makers? One of the girls stands up to peer at the mattress. One wonders what she sees, or hears? At one time, life happened on that mattress, as on most mattresses; and also death. The older man tugs at the girl's sleeve but still she stands. The world she lives in, one understands, is a safer planet for the Rule of Law— the League of Nations blooming out of the Great War, the United Nations blossoming from World War II, and now, in this tiny corner of the earth, the droning stillness of Romiti's courtroom somehow connected to the "War on Gangs." Street crime. Long knives flashing in the night. But just then, it seems, the only evidence worth making known in this room would be the sounds of death and life that took place on that mattress, or even the memory of those sounds—although one realizes they were spoken in a different language than the language spoken here.

The girl sits down. Zimmers and Cedarquist are now talking about a piece of plasterboard:

"Would you please describe Exhibit No. 119?"

"It is a piece of plasterboard."

"Is there anything unusual about the plasterboard?"

"It is a piece of plasterboard with an elongated hole or slashmark."

"Did you examine the hole or slashmark?"

"Yes, I did . . ."

And then the day is over. The Sheriff's aides come in and drag the mattress out, placing it first on its side, and then pulling it into the corridor, where it will be taken back to the warehouse. Cedarquist helps put the mattress into a warehouse box. He seems a nice man, although tired just then. He puts on his coat and starts stuffing papers into a briefcase.

It's hard to know about the way that any of us connects with the past, with his past, or with common events that happened—how much does any of us remember? And how much did any of us ever know? Fred Hampton's mattress is an object now (as it always was), floating in time and space—it is nowhere now, except where it is: on the floor of a courtroom, or in a box in a warehouse. And Hampton, where is he—other than dead? And his friends? And the police, whose lives coincided with theirs that early morning? The police are also in the courtroom now. The friends are dead or scattered, although Deborah Johnson takes her small child to visit with Hampton's parents once a month. We are here, too.

Each tick of the clock, as we well know, is a point in

time. And each point in time, as soon as it has happened, not so much vanishes as alters, shifts in appearance, form, specific gravity. Where were you the night the *Titanic* went down? The day Kennedy was shot? Pearl Harbor? The Fall of Constantinople? Even historians seem scarcely able to answer such questions, and rarely try—this is not a nation, after all, which sets huge value on a sense of connection with the past, the actual as opposed to the sentimental past. The moment is over. Now we are in a new moment. We were never in the old moment. Now, the new moment is over. We are in another moment . . . Thus we avoid the drag of mortality, do we not? Unlike the morbid, death-fond ancients, with their garrulous old men, and harps, and reeds, and quavery singsong to tell us of the sack of Troy, the rape of villages, the deeds of men and gods, to tell us of death and life, and life and death—we move nimbly, eyes ahead; we watch the evening news, and collect seashells, and snapshots, and avoid death and other matters.

We are *here* now. We seem quite sure of that. We sit in a certain room, or stand on a certain street. Question: Where were you then? Answer: I was home. In my room. I was watching the rain fall on the empty street. Question: Where were you the day President Kennedy was shot? Answer: I was in a bus going to work. I remember I was going to work late because I had just been to the dentist. Question: Where were you in the early morning of December 4, 1969? I was home. I watched the rain fall on the empty street. I was driving in an unmarked police car, heading west. I was lying in bed, watching shadows on the ceiling, dreaming heated dreams, feeling cold, hearing noises on the staircase . . . There is no telling what any of us might really know today, if we but knew where we had been.

A short while ago in a newspaper interview, President Nixon called for an end to "the whole era of permissiveness," and since Mr. Nixon is rarely a man to go against the grain, one imagines he is on to something. Nearly a year ago, in fact, *Vogue* was telling *its* constituents that the fashion for radical and outlandish costumes was past, and that we were entering something called the New Elegance. In literature we have had *Love Story*. MGM has just given us *The Great Waltz*—the story of Johann Strauss. This year's college class, it is noted approvingly by college presidents, is well behaved and serious. The kids attend classes. There is an increase in fraternity rushing. A book about a seagull has been selling millions of copies. Was it ever different?

President Nixon certainly doesn't seem to have changed much in the last few years—nor indeed (one guesses) have many of the people in Judge Romiti's courtroom. Mr. Hanrahan's hair is perhaps a trifle longer than he might have worn it at Notre Dame, but not by much. Barnabas Sears, as always, wears a white shirt to work. A couple of the younger police defendants have longish sideburns and even a mustache or two, but then so do many Military Policemen, and Spiro Agnew's son-in-law. Still atop Chicago, Mayor Daley seems much the same.

Older, maybe more tractable. Chicago seems much the same, except for the taller buildings.

And what of Camelot, which Mayor Daley helped provide us with his legerdemain among the Cook County precincts, because even in 1960—despite the dash of the New Frontier and the elegances of Camelot Jack, despite the talk of how the center of the country had moved, had shifted—back in that November virtually half of the same country then had wished Mr. Nixon President? For a while anyway Camelot stood before us. The Queen ordered Paris clothes. The Prince played Hotspur football. The Air Force Band no longer strummed Eisenhower waltzes into the ears of visiting Norwegian monarchs—instead the young King would ask the best and oldest of the world's great cellists to play a little lovely Schumann and interesting Bach for a few hours after dinner in the East Room.

And if there was not as much political motion in the country as some people thought, if perhaps this center of the nation had not magically moved from Canton, Ohio, to some exquisite midpoint between Cambridge and Washington, there was still a definite motion of a certain kind—and as a guess one would say that it was mostly sexual: a kind of sexual frothing-up in America, occasioned partly by the sudden coming-of-age of millions of kids—liberal-educated, no-nonsense smart kids, taught by their parents to think themselves and their feelings (those feelings we would all hear so much about) important; and partly by the much-harangued sexual repressiveness of American society, which, it turns out, was not much more repressed than most other Western nations, but where a gap had increasingly formed, and made itself visible, between private sexual life and the vast omnipresent secular sexuality of the outside world.

This sexual frothing didn't create the New Music, or the New Clothes, or the New Politics (any more than Camelot Jack had created the sexual frothing), but somehow it all worked together, one came out of the other, was somehow entwined with the other. Suddenly (or so it seemed), in the 1960s, men and women were discussing the most extraordinary aspects of their private lives—in private and in groups. A strident new music was playing. Profanity, especially sexual profanity—which had caused books to be banned by the courts—became a part of everyday speech. Anything sexual was now (especially) published in books. Women of thirty and under, and thirty and over, wore aggressively short skirts. Men wore strangely colored ties on strangely colored shirts, or borrowed sexually attractive costumes from other periods or vocations: work clothes, cowboy leather, Indian beads.

And all the time the kids were in the vanguard. The kids: those myriad, ever-present, extremely visible, now explicitly sexual shapes. Once we had told them to be what they wanted to be, to act how they wanted to act, we had made up beguiling movie and literary fables about the evils of conformity. Now, they were upstairs in the guest room making love with a "close friend," somebody really cool, and afterwards coming downstairs to chat about blowing up the bank Dad worked in; and we hated it all, and felt helpless, and felt attracted by it. After all, our immortality was with them. Housewives hemmed their skirts higher, and made strange confidences in "group." Dad grew his hair longer, bought some shirts, took the secretary on a business trip to Seattle—where he confessed his real ambition was to quit the bank and do good work in the ghetto.

And *protest*. The War, at first or mostly. The environment. Universities. The draft. Big business. Business. Grapes. Squareness. Hubert Humphrey. Troop trains. Napalm. Sexual freedom. Racial Inequality. Marriage. The Church. The Establishment—everything that wasn't young and free and equal and full of feeling was the Establishment. We reacted to this protest according to our own differing lines of parent-child tensions, which is to say that some—purposive uncertain liberals—tried to "manage" their own feelings (never too well thought out in the first place) and followed in the path of the children; and others—equally purposive, more fearful of the tribal young, determined to be certain about one damned thing in this life—said No. Said: to Hell with your Vermont hills, or New Mexico burrows, or cloisters, or music alcoves, or far-out trips. Said: I am here, and you are there (wherever you are), and you will not be able to stay *there* long, because the only food you have you have from me, and I never gave you out enough for traveling.

And so today it is late autumn, 1972. Chicago: a sturdy midland city, a city (as with most hereabouts) that has more past than it knows what to do with. Mr. Nixon is still with us. Mr. Daley is still with us. The bricks of the city are much the same. And the people—well, it is hard to know about the people.

Four years ago, Mr. Nixon was first in the White House. Some pictures swim briefly, strangely into view. The face of Mayor Daley cursing Senator Ribicoff at the 1968 Convention. The TV interviews with Abbie Hoffman. College kids swarming the streets with their petitions to end the war. A curious far-off time: girls in those short short dresses. Girls in cutout dresses. Artists walking in picket lines outside museums. Strange art: Geometry. Marilyn Monroe. A plaster figure in a phone booth.

In Los Angeles, then, Charles Manson was on trial. And in Chicago—to "support" the Conspiracy 7—the SDS "Weathermen" staged a march, a rampage one November day: thirty or forty pale, wild-eyed young men and women, wearing motorcycle crash helmets, running down Michigan Avenue, smashing store windows and car windows, getting slammed by the police. One remembers, too, a reporter describing a brief exchange between Fred Hampton and one of the "Weathermen," who had been urging Hampton to bring his Panthers in on the march. "If we did something like that, they'd just shoot us," said Hampton, who was younger than most of the "Weathermen," and not really such a very big deal in the Panthers—not big on the level of, say, Bobby Seale, who was being as macho as he could in Judge Hoffman's courtroom and getting into *Time* magazine and the Cook County Jail as a result.

There has been talk lately of how the nation now is weary from Vietnam. There is talk of getting back to the business of the country. Business is in fact improving. A brokerage house announces that for the first time in years it is recommending steel stocks. Time moves, and then moves, and then moves. One wonders now, because it *is* now, and there is a pale sun on the buildings, and people are walking by in the street, if the country is indeed wearied from Vietnam, or from anything (except possibly from that strain of having had to seem sexual)—or if it is that we would simply not look at it any more, would not, will not, could not stand to look at it any more because looking at it (as strange McGovern willed us to do) compels us to look on that in ourselves which we cannot bear to look at. *We know (as we always knew). We are actually doing what we are doing.* Later, we will somehow order it. Even if we find mounds of graves or charred-out villages, we will somehow order it. We will organize reconstruction programs. The town of Hanoi, West Virginia, will help rebuild Hanoi, North Vietnam, and there will be exchange visits of policemen on Christmas Day. Maybe it happened, but it is not happening now. The moment is over.

But for one wild, brief period of time—was it three or four or two years ago? was it this year? ever?—we nearly looked at it. As we nearly looked at the anger of black people—the anger which came from the same source as the craters in Indo-China. From us. Since that moment, there have been changes. The children, or many of them, have come back down from the hills. We have lowered our skirts. Raised our sideburns. Proclaimed that we are a bit wearied and preoccupied, and leaving a number of dead behind us and some strange disconnected memories—a mattress in a warehouse, a cutout dress hanging in a closet somewhere—we are moving back to the business of the country. It seems odd, and faraway, and not quite believable that we were ever anywhere else.

A ND now as to Robert Zimmers, also astride our present—the ace FBI examiner, the astronaut-expert, the
prosecution's Man of Science (whose own past had contained such triumphs as the Clutter—*In Cold Blood*
case)—it is hard to see what his near-endless testimony
has evoked in anyone beyond boredom; and not a trivial
boredom either, the kind which often brings out the true
seriousness of other experts, somehow beckoning them
to dive beneath the jargon and detail and attend to the
deep mysteries below. Zimmers and Cedarquist together,
each with the best of intentions, seem to have created
between them a boredom of real and almost dangerous
proportions, a boredom far beyond the quaint, bluebottle-
fly boredom of Dickensian courts—a dry, rainless, flyless,

quaintless boredom such as perhaps is only found elsewhere by soldiers in peacetime, sitting stupefied with
heat and blankness in the middle of a Fort Benning summer, while a training sergeant (another tanned, mono-
tone technician) discourses on the assembly of an automatic rifle, or the disassembly, or on trigger pins, or
armatures, or how to pitch a tent, and with how many
pegs. Had Judge Romiti, more withdrawn with each
session, less patient, ever been in the Army and been
instructed by an ROTC lieutenant on how to clean the
M-1 rifle?

Zimmers, to be sure, seems to have painstakingly done
what has been asked of him—has methodically enumer-
ated and attested to and described the various shell
casings and bullet holes and recovered bullets and recovered pellets; and it is clear (although no clearer than
it was on the mock-up) that there had been a lot of them,
and that they had all—all but one, anyway—come from
police weapons. He has even, somewhere amid his
recitations, acknowledged it as his opinion that the Police
Firearms Examiner, Sadunas, who had mistaken two
police shotgun shells for shells from Brenda Harris' gun,
could not have reached this conclusion as a routine mistake. He took up the disputed question of the fields-of-
fire—the police, after all, still claimed that the Panthers
had fired at them repeatedly, but only one Panther bullet
had been found. "Could a person," Cedarquist would in-
tone, "lying on that bed in that room . . . holding a
shotgun loaded with .oo shot . . . pointing it and dis-
charging it toward doors 3, 2, and 1 . . . could a person
firing that shotgun fire it in such a way that the shot might

exit the apartment without leaving impact points anywhere inside in the apartment?" And so forth. "No," says Robert Zimmers. "Not in my opinion. No." And so forth.

In the end, though, it all comes to seem increasingly like a dialogue between umpires after one of those military war games. Did the Red team actually obliterate point K.12 and then capture the Blue airstrip with their tank battalion, or had the Blue team, with its amphibious landing at L.22, already destroyed the Red tank column . . . ? All along, for nearly three years now, metaphor has been piled upon metaphor, metaphors of ballistic evidence seeking to explain, or deny, or support metaphors of investigation—as if in some as yet unrevealed arrangement of bullets and bullet holes and shell casings and lines of fire some magic truth were to be arrived at. Now, the prosecution staff, and old Zimmers, all of them working like hell, busy as bees or beavers, pile detail upon detail—as if this mountainous accumulation of evidence (wondrous evidence!) will finally lead somebody (God? Judge Romiti? The outside world which by now is so disinterested that newspapers barely send reporters anymore?) to draw a deep coherent conclusion about the event; when, as things stand, the prosecution, and the Judge, and in fact the operable Law, are all quite acceptably connected together by a language that admits of no deep and magic meanings, no depths beneath the detail and jargon, no depths where anyone might swim, except for some brief and private amusement.

The defense then produces its own stupefying charts—

mainly a floor plan of the Monroe Street apartment, which defense lawyers place over the grey mock-up, with its metal dowels still in place, still indicating the multitude of bullets which had entered the several rooms. The floor plan is of white cardboard, showing the layout of the rooms, and imposed on this layout are various strips of colored tape: orange, yellow, green, purple. The colored tapes stretch between various doorways and windows and positions within the apartment. It is the defense's contention that the numerous but unrecovered Panther shots all sped out of the windows and out through the doors, or else had hidden themselves in bundles of clothes—Panther bullets apparently whooshing and thudding into stacks of laundry, where they presumably lay unobserved in Panther trouser cuffs and Panther shirtings, later to be lost or removed or hidden by enemies of the state—or in this instance, since the state was bringing the case, by enemies of the State's Attorney's police.

It somehow seems a fitting final view of the event. A picture of tiny windows, half-opened doors. The dead of night. Police with carbines and machine guns and shotguns. Panther sharpshooters, crouched behind their poster and coloring book barricades, firing with deadly aim into *infinity*—bullets zipping through the narrow doorways and out across the horizon, picked up eventually perhaps by distant villagers in far-off lands, tossed carelessly into mountain streams; or else dispersed in laundry bundles.

What *had* been the event? "But tell me, sir," says lawyer John Coghlan, the ex-policeman, "can you say without *any* reasonable doubt that it was impossible for a bullet, fired from the southeast corner of the living room, to follow the path of the orange field-of-fire and exit from the back doorway?" Zimmers, very testy by then: "I don't think it was possible." Coghlan, stentorian: "Sir, I am asking you about *reasonable doubt.* Can you say without any *reasonable doubt . . . ?*" Zimmers: "I have found no evidence to—" Coghlan: "Sir, that is not the question. The question is about *reasonable doubt.*" Zimmers: "I cannot say without *any* doubt at all because—" Coghlan: "Thank you very much."

In the end, clearly the trial has been the event. And the trial is soon to be over. Zimmers is the last witness for the prosecution. "I think Zimmers wrapped it up for us," says Wayland Cedarquist, who is beginning to look as white in the face as Sears. "I think he helped us bring out all the pertinent facts." The defense, as has been expected, now puts in a motion for an acquittal. Judge Romiti says that he will spend the weekend reviewing all the evidence, and will listen to final arguments on Monday.

THEN over the weekend, the sky strangely darkens. Is it a real event? A true happening? In any case, a press conference is called in the Civic Center by Hanrahan, by Police Superintendent Conlisk, and by Cook County Sheriff Richard Elrod, and there it is announced by the triumvirate that seven young men—seven young black men—have been arrested in connection with nine murders, including two "multiple killings" in the Chicago suburbs.

The murders, which took place in unconnected areas some months ago, seemed gratuitous and nasty enough, and the young suspects, when they become visible on their way to jail, look darkly sullen and angry—all of it a vaguely familiar scenario, down to the fact that the suspects have been held incommunicado for forty-eight hours by the Sheriff's police until the time of the press conference.

But what really adds a special dark note (and a more definite feeling of having been here before) is the official statement, which seems less concerned with stating, or even alleging a definite connection between the suspects and the various murders, than it is with announcing that the young blacks had been members of a just-discovered, secret, nationwide, terror Army of black Vietnam veterans called De Mau Mau. Declares Sheriff Elrod: "It appears as if they were roaming the countryside looking for someone to kill." He is asked by reporters if the murders seemed racially motivated. "I can see no other apparent motivation," he says. "This was an organized gang. We have the ringleaders. We have the primary trigger-men. These men were motivated to commit brutal crimes. Yes, the primary motivation seems to have been racial."

State's Attorney Hanrahan, whose re-election race against Bernard Carey is running increasingly close, seems, as he poses for pictures alongside Elrod and Conlisk—the three defenders of Rome—more of a public presence than he has been in weeks or months. His face is stern. His manner purposeful. "Yes," he says, "we have sufficient evidence to sustain the charges that have been brought. We do not intend to tell you what that is." He says: "I think you ought to take your hats off to the Police Department and the Sheriff's investigators. This is an example of the highest caliber police work."

Superintendent Conlisk, the grave shepherd of his city,

again speaks softly and almost inaudibly. "The Chicago Police Department was a proud member of this fine team," he says, "and it manifests the kind of relationships which exist between and among the various agencies in the administration of criminal justice here. It is definitely a happy event for the people of this county."

Happy event or not, by Monday morning the four Chicago papers (whose own attraction for the dark shadow seems equal to the occasion) are full of little else. "NINE KILLINGS CHARGED TO GANG," says the *Tribune* in a relatively conservative headline. "MAU MAU GANG: 8 TIED TO MASS MURDERS," says the *Sun-Times.* "REPORT MASS KILLER GANG PLOTTED TO SLAY COPS HERE," says the *Daily News.* By Monday afternoon, *Chicago Today* announces: "MURDER GANG 3000 STRONG."

It seems an eerie moment, or rather an eerie memory of a moment because it shortly fades away. But for an odd blink of time, there once again is Edward Hanrahan and the police—but especially Hanrahan—engaged in battle on the citizens' behalf; and there somewhere, beyond the horizon, or as a sinister cloud moving toward the city, or roaming the streets, once again is the dark specter. And there too are our tribunes, the reporters and the newscasters, once again taking dictation from the guardians of the city.

"The De Mau Mau organization," reports *Chicago Today,* "has been described by officials in the State's Attorney's Office and the Police Department as 'a bunch of aimless revolutionaries who hit white people usually after they get high on pot.'" The *Sun-Times* says: "Police spokesmen state that the gang may number between 50

166

and 75 persons in the Chicago area, and may well be responsible for unsolved murders in other states." *Chicago Today* says: "The De Mau Mau gang is a black organization with a core of Vietnam veterans trained to kill in combat . . . the name is derived from that of the Mau Mau terrorist movement against whites in Kenya, Africa . . . Police investigators here say the group has a nationwide membership of 3000." The *Daily News* reports an "official informant" as saying that there were "from 300 to 400 members of De Mau Mau in the Chicago area, and from 3000 to 4000 across the nation. According to a high police authority, the black terrorist gang planned to begin systematically killing white policemen."

And then once again, in due course, some other voices come to be heard—although not on the front pages of the newspapers. The president of the black college, where some of the suspects had attended, says that he had heard of De Mau Mau: it was a small veterans group of about a dozen members, one of many larger veterans groups at his college. Leaders of a national black veterans organization say that although the suspects might indeed have committed the murders, De Mau Mau had nothing to do with it, in fact hardly existed, and that black veterans have enough troubles as it is. Civil liberties lawyers criticize Elrod and Hanrahan for holding the suspects so long before charging them. The Sheriff's police chief, who headed the investigation, acknowledges that the only information *he* had ever received about the De Mau Mau before making the arrests had been from "random street talk." Finally, a "Pentagon spokesman" surfaces and says that, to the Army's knowledge, a casual loosely knit group called De Mau Mau (the word itself a corruption of the Vietnamese-GI expression "di di mau," meaning "move fast") had existed in Vietnam a few years before, consisting of about fifty marines, including whites, and had then been mainly for the purpose of improving race relations.

But by then it is one week later, and the story has largely evaporated from the papers. The suspects are still arraigned and are presumably in some kind of trouble, although no one is bothering about them much any more, and the original evidence linking them to the murders still seems as thin as ever. The sinister De Mau Mau meanwhile has vanished—three thousand well-organized, racially berserk black killers disappearing into the catacombs of Chicago as silently as they had appeared. Once again the dark shadow has been summoned, has in fact rushed into our midst—one forgets how quickly it can rush, and into what welcoming arms. And then has vanished, faded back into a dream.

"Even if the suspects turn out to be guilty," says a suddenly sober editorial, "it is not entirely clear at this point whether the motives in the killings were purely racial, or whether De Mau Mau existed at all . . ." But, before that point of sobriety and self-awareness, it is Monday. A Monday in court. Hanrahan wears a stern centurion's expression, and a new striped tie, to Room 702.

I n the courtroom, the press and visitors rows are once again crowded. Reporters exchange the latest communiques from the De Mau Mau front, or carry them under their arms in the form of headlines. Marshals stroll up and down in the aisle, greeting the police defendants, and questioning press credentials. A few black men are in the courtroom, mainly reporters—allowed in after many explications and displays of press passes. Outside, in the corridor, a group of half a dozen young black men stand around, drinking courthouse cafeteria coffee in plastic cups, and waiting to be allowed in, which they never are.

The defense arguments begin with Thomas Sullivan, dressed in a serious suit, who first proffers Judge Romiti a list of case references he has compiled, pertaining to the defense motion for an acquittal on the basis of un-proven charges, and then proceeds to bring up once more the Panthers' predilection for violence, their antisocial habits, and their dishonesty as indicated by the changed testimony—a revelation, as he now construes it, that had been extracted from an unwilling, and probably dis-honest, prosecution by the aggressive, truth-seeking tac-tics of the defense.

Sullivan expresses indignation at the recent travail of the defendants. Not only had they been doing their job, attempting to safeguard the community from the forays of armed desperadoes, but in this case the armed desperadoes had been "sworn enemies" of society. He mentions the Panther coloring book once again. He speaks of the bravery of the State's Attorney's police.

Sullivan is followed by John Coghlan. The courtroom is by now silent and attentive. Judge Romiti no longer makes notes upon his yellow pad, but gazes before him with a fine expression of judicial gravity.

Says John Coghlan: "You know, we all understand—as men and as policemen—that it's open season these days on policemen, and they know it from the day they put on that star."

And: "There's only one way that I know of for a copper to prove that he's on the square and that is to die."

And: "There's a funny thing about being a policeman. The laymen don't understand it. Few newsmen ever un-derstand it. And few judges understand it. A policeman has the same fears for his life that any of the rest of us have. But he has one more thing that only a policeman understands, and that is: if he goes yellow on his partners he is through on the job. He never gets another partner."

And: "I'll tell you right now that we wouldn't be here today if Officer Davis had taken a shotgun deer slug through the belly as he went through that door."

And: "When Joe Gorman followed him with his machine gun, he didn't know what he was going to find in there. There was action, there was shooting, there was darkness. But Joe Gorman knows that if he doesn't go through that door, he is through as a policeman. He'll never be able to hold up his head again. And he'd sooner die."

And: "If Duke Davis hadn't been bent over, with that alley-wise cunning that comes from twenty years on the force, part of him would have been up there on the stairway. He'd have proved then he was an honorable man."

And: "In this town, about the only way a copper can prove he is an honorable man is by dying."

And then comes Edward Hanrahan, who has three lawyers in attendance but is acting here as his own counsel. He, too, is dressed solemnly for the occasion, and seems visibly moved by Coghlan's dithyrambs on the dangerous and comradely life of policemen. As he strides toward the bench—a stocky man in a dark suit—he passes by Coghlan and pats him on the shoulder.

"I have sat here, your honor," says Hanrahan, "for thirteen long weeks in silence, and it certainly hasn't been easy.

"We have listened to the philosophy of the Black Panther Party, brought out on the witness stand by the prosecution's very own witnesses, talking about the mandates that every member of that organization have a gun, be able to use it, and know how to defend his pad.

"We listened this morning to Mr. Sullivan recall the testimony of Deborah Johnson when she related the poem by Fred Hampton—that revolting poem—expressing satisfaction from killing a police officer. I was repelled by it then, and more so this morning when it was brought back to my memory.

"And when I listened to that evidence, and I think about Duke Davis and these other officers—well, I believe that the people of Cook County owe a medal to every one of those officers who had the integrity to go into that apartment under fire to seize those weapons, which, if the Black Panther philosophy had been allowed to continue in force, would undoubtedly have been used to kill other people, to kill other Gilhoolys and Rappaports . . .

"I say again that I have been proud to be associated with these police officers and believe they deserve the thanks of the community for what they did that evening . . . Neither I nor any of the defendants have committed any crime, and there has been no evidence at all to contradict that statement . . .

"In fact, this is an outlandish case . . . and how easy it is to make these false allegations, and how difficult to disprove the falsity—that is so easily leveled at men who have no defense except that they come here to trial, or else die.

"Thank God, Duke Davis *did* use his twenty-four years of police know-how to come in low. Thank God, Joe Gorman *did* have the guts to follow him. And thank God for men like Ed Carmody, who don't duck out for coffee when there's a fire fight going on.

"If we didn't have policemen like this in our city, neither you nor I would have any degree of safety at all, especially when that kind of philosophy is spewed from the witness stand by persons who have no concern for the truth at all, and no concern and confidence in our system—except that perhaps they can pervert it, and they came awfully close here . . ."

There is more, a lot more. On the disputed Panther statements that Cedarquist had turned over to the defense: "What kind of search for truth would close its eyes to that vital information? Of course, the hiding of that evidence is completely consistent with the objective and philosophies of the Black Panther Party." On Barnabas Sears: "I suggest the worst failure of all has been the failure of the special prosecutor to follow his own repeated declarations . . . and protect the rights of the defendants." On criticisms of the raid published afterward in the press: "These irresponsible statements that undermined public confidence in law enforcement . . ."

Finally, the other defense lawyers slip a note to Hanrahan telling him that time is running out. He glances up furiously at the clock, as if, were he to look hard enough at it, it would stop.

Then more softly: "Your honor, the evidence in this case will show that . . . all of the defendants must be discharged . . . Also this indictment should never have been returned in the first place . . . And even an acquittal will never undo the uncalculable damage to the reputation of every police officer and every defendant in this room.

"But worse than that: even an acquittal may not sufficiently resolve the doubts that have been created in the minds of so many people about the integrity of law enforcement in Cook County. And I suggest that *that's* the real and unending tragedy in this case."

It is Barnabas Sears's turn the next day, and he seems to have spruced himself up for the occasion—his suit seems pressed, his necktie is in place, his hair is combed. His face is a bit pinker, too.

He speaks in good voice also—his voice stronger than it has been, his delivery measured. His daughter, a red-haired woman in her thirties, sits in one of the rows behind the press. Sears smiles at her before beginning his argument. He looks quite gallant this morning.

Still, it is all a somehow quaint and almost perverse performance, although whose fault that it is would be hard to say. Coghlan and Hanrahan and the other defense lawyers have been theatrical, but within the context of a particular myth: the gallant policemen, or rather, cops, as saviors of our society . . . brave guardians . . . Duke Davis (known to virtually every city reporter as one of the meanest men on the force) "coming in low," . . . the disgusting Panthers and their "philosophy."

Sears is now also theatrical, but he has no competing myth on his side.

At the outset, in fact, he seems anxious to divest himself of the only one he might have had, this same *Pantherism*, the disease so often mentioned by the defense—Sears apparently accepting their version of it as a disease, as if, could he but prove he did not have it himself, he might then go on to more important matters of law and evidence. "Your honor," he declares in what is now a fine, full, midwestern voice (and it is not, after all, an odd social point of view for a seventy-year-old, white, midwestern lawyer to have), "I suppose the next thing I will hear from the defense is that I have some communion with Panthers. Well, I will tell you, your honor, I was born out in southeastern North Dakota . . ." He is not disowning them, of course, or challenging their right to exist. He is not an armed oppressor, a vengeful conqueror, like some others—perhaps more a missionary, a goodly Episcopalian just returned from the Zambesi. ". . . And my dad was admitted to practice in the Territory of Dakota. That was in 1888, and he was then old enough to be my grandfather. And I have some of his July 4th speeches still among my most treasured possessions . . . and those speeches said that everybody stood equal before the law, that however high or low, one of the glories of the American Republic (he always used the word Republic) was that it protected the *weak* as well as the strong, the *despised* as well as the admired . . ."

A decent man, Sears clearly is. His heart is in South Dakota, or downstate Illinois, or maybe home on Lake Shore Drive. His mind is in the Law. One imagined him, say, a colonel in the postwar Army, receiving Harry Truman's order to integrate, and that very afternoon issuing the orders to his command, not batting an eye. "Gentlemen, I have my orders. You have yours." And would there be more than that? Well, what more than that had Harry Truman wanted?

And now in Judge Romiti's courtroom, having absolved himself of communion with Pantherism, having not forsaken his poor black flock upon the Zambesi but, hopefully, having assured his London congregation that he had not gone native—Sears takes us once again into the Law.

For a whole morning he lists cases. He quotes cases. Perry. Dustin. State of Illinois. 470. People vs. Ogden. 326. Walczak. Shields. United States vs. O'Brien. 162. 245. Edwards. Keegan. Greenway vs. Maryland. The cases are primarily to support the prosecution's claim that there had been enough evidence presented to sustain a guilty verdict, and that the burden of proof was on the court to recognize a conspiracy had taken place. "When three or more people enter into an agreement or agreements, etc. . . ." Sears unreels pages of source quotations. Somehow, the Conspiracy Laws, whether dating from 1782 or 1968, seem no less distasteful than before.

Romiti takes down all the case references on his yellow pad, but seems colder and more withdrawn with each new enumeration—here after all is the former Dean of the De Paul Law School, his look seems to be saying, once again being lectured to and bored by this elderly lawyer. "I call your honor's attention to the fact that . . ."

And: "As I am sure your honor remembers, but permit me to refresh his recollection . . ."

And then Sears takes us once again into the evidence. He does it well, too—more coherently at any rate than he and his staff have mostly managed in dealing with the witnesses; the facts more clearly linked to some visible point of view, and not so many of them. But it is too late now, and, besides, evidence in a final argument is not the same as evidence transmitted from the witness stand.

Sears recounts the various State's Attorney's press conferences in the days after the raid, and with every quoted paragraph, with every righteous and furious assertion by the State's Attorney during that December, one has a glimpse back into the angers and hysteria of that time—with today's new De Mau Mau headlines to reinforce the ironies, should that be necessary. Although by now the trial is over. One can tell it by the easy indifference of most of the defendants. One can tell it by Romiti's impatience. One can tell it especially in the mood of the defense table. They know they have it won.

A "conspiracy to obstruct justice" supposedly is hard enough to prove in the most favorable of contexts, but here the defense has owned the context, has owned it all along. Who, after all, were these defendants but young men, men in their prime, supported not only by official regulations (always a help), but by their own sense of rectitude, of mission, of comradeship (and the regard which white male society has for comradeship, at least among white males), sustained in the end by the emotional apparat of the whole close world they live in— which came to include, finally, the prosecution.

And Sears, who seems to belong more to that same world every moment he speaks, with every learned declamation, with every civilized irony he utters, is not young, is what is called past his prime, has become old, has become old perhaps in the course of the trial. White hair, white face. It has not turned out to be another Summerdale, another Darrowesque gallop against a gang of TV-stealing policemen, bad cops. This one has been different, altogether different. At the start, doubtless, the prosecution had had a sense of outrage on its side, a kind of mission—although mostly directed toward the Law. Since then, mainly there have been facts, and evidence, and records, and examinations, and re-examinations, which is what the Law is supposed to be about; but no sustaining myth. And what does a lawyer, a priest of the Law, need with myths?

In the final moments of the trial, the defense lawyers harry Sears as one might an old bull.

Sears: . . . In the interest of accuracy, and to serve as memoranda, I will refer to this article . . .

Defense: We object!

Sears: If you will *please* . . .

Defense: The *article* was not admitted!

Romiti: I don't think the article was admitted.

Defense: And for him to say "for the sake of accuracy!"

Romiti: The court has fully read the transcript. The court is fully aware of it. There is no need to go into it further.

Sears: I was just referring to it for the purpose of refreshing my recollection.

Defense: Your honor, this is another deception!

Romiti: Please sit down.

Sears: I trust the court doesn't think I intended deception.

Romiti: No, but I have read the transcripts within the past three days. Proceed from that point.

Sears: Well now. Perhaps the most striking statement that appears in the article . . .

Defense: Objection to anything in the article!

Romiti: Did the witness testify to this?

Sears: Yes, he did.

Romiti: Go ahead.

Sears: I have to check my notes on the witness . . .

Defense: If he has to check his notes, he shouldn't be saying it.

And so forth.

Sears speaks for the better part of two days—a stocky, white-haired figure, his feet apart, standing there beneath the Judge. The Judge looks cold. The defense lawyers behind him fidget, smile, call out objections. Sears travels once again—the last time—through the old, old story: an ancient tale now, from another time. "Thus, at an absolute minimum, the police defendants claim that the occupants fired at them as follows . . ." And: "However, the physical facts and the evidence identify only *one* shot . . ." And: "The police defendants say that shots were fired at them from locations from which it is physically impossible to fire projectiles without hitting apartment walls . . ." And then it is over.

Hanrahan gets briskly to his feet and grips Tom Sullivan's hand, and then John Coghlan's. Officer Davis stretches, and says something to Gorman which makes him laugh. Sears looks back at his daughter, and smiles at her, and goes to get his overcoat. Judge Romiti says that he will announce his verdict in two days, on Wednesday.

Wednesday, November 1, 1972, the courtroom is packed. Outside in the corridor, visitors mill around, while large black Sheriff's aides stop nearly everyone, although in fact mostly women television artists and black reporters, searching handbags and pockets and credentials as if something dangerous and notable were in the air—a sudden last-ditch juridical uprising by the De Mau Mau, or perhaps the hijacking of the entire courtroom to some distant and repellent land.

Inside, there are still few blacks, except for five or six black journalists, but all the rows are filled, mainly with friends and relatives and children of the defendants, and by the press, Chicago and national, which has returned in force. The atmosphere is a bit like a graduation of some sort. The police defendants all seem to be wearing their best suits, and walk about beside their table with well-scrubbed looks, and neckties properly tied, and eager, quite boyish smiles. The defense lawyers are even jollier, a bit like coaches of a winning team mingling with the players before the annual awards ceremonies. Hanrahan talks to his brother, Richard. The wives and children sit together in rows, pleasant housewife ladies in their Sunday coats and dresses, some hats and gloves, many children also dressed for Sunday.

Then Judge Romiti enters. Everybody rises, with much formality and respect for the Law. Romiti looks grave, and is no longer wearing the orange shirt beneath his robes. The clerk of the court, a stocky Irishman, also suitably dressed for the occasion in a light blue suit, reads out the list of defendants, who answer present.

Then Romiti, seated now at the bench, takes out a piece of paper and begins to read:

"This court might normally be inclined to rule on this motion without comment. However, as has been pointed out many times during the course of this trial, this is a most unusual case . . . This court is aware, painfully so, that this is one of those 'you're damned if you do and damned if you don't' cases. The only question is which way one is going to be damned . . .

"I must confess, human nature being what it is, that there exists the temptation to take what might appear to be a course of least resistance. However, being mindful of the strictures and duties of judges, to do so in this case would be an abrogation by this court of its duties . . ."

By this time, the entire crowded courtroom is in absolute silence. The smiles have gone from the defendants. Reporters who have bet 100 to 1 since the beginning of the trial that there was no chance of Romiti not acquitting Hanrahan et al. exchange perplexed glances. What does he mean—not take the path of least resistance?

Up on the bench, Judge Romiti—wondrously solemn and judgelike—continues his reading:

"Judicial canons provide that . . . a judge should be unswayed by partisan interests . . . or by public clamor or fear of criticism. In short, this court has a duty to all charged with crimes, whatever their position or status, to be certain that all rights are protected . . . To do anything less than that in this case would be judicially improper and intellectually dishonest as well . . ."

And then he suddenly turns down the homestretch:

"It is not the issue before this court to determine who fired which weapon, how many times and from what physical part of the apartment . . . It is not the purpose of this trial . . . to attempt to assess or evaluate the work and conduct of the involved officers, nor to offer any critique thereon . . . For four full days the court was on the receiving end of a great volume of rhetoric, oratory, some histrionics and emotional appeals . . . The court must also note a difference between inferences, about which so much has been said, and speculation and conjecture with which this case is so replete . . ."

And then: ". . . After a thorough review and careful analysis and consideration of the totality of the evidence, including the testimony given by defendants before the various bodies before which they appeared . . . this court can only conclude and does conclude that evidence is not sufficient to establish or prove any conspiracy against any defendant . . . A judgment of acquittal is entered as to each defendant and each defendant is discharged."

And that is it. Indictment Number 71-1791 is at last finished with, terminated, disposed of. Several of the defendants raise their hands in victory salutes. There are loud cheers, and laughter, and some wifely sobs from among the visitors. Romiti, still splendidly judgelike, sails from the noise-filled room by the back door. Hanrahan announces a press conference. Sears hands out a short typewritten statement which says something about "respect for the law and maintenance of our juridical system is essential for our survival as a free society," and puts on his overcoat, because it is still cold outside, and his homburg hat, which looks quite natty, and walks slowly out through the crowd in Room 702.

Over by what has been the prosecution's table, Howard Savage, one of the two black attorneys, stands up, then kicks his chair halfway across the room, but no one notices. John Coghlan has his arms around two of the policemen's wives and jokes with several reporters. Then everybody leaves. In the back of the room, while Romiti had read his verdict, Bill Hampton—Fred Hampton's older brother—had been sitting, a tall, large black young man of about twenty-six, wearing a raincoat; and now he stands near the doorway, and people walk by him as they go out, and it is hard to tell whether he wants to speak to them or not to speak to them. Wayland Cedarquist goes by him, and the policemen, and their wives and children, and the defense lawyers, and the reporters, and then a young black television sketcher comes up and says something to him, and Bill Hampton leans over, because the sketcher is quite short and Bill Hampton is well over six feet, and nods his head or says something in reply, and then they both walk together toward the elevators.

Said Edward Hanrahan: "Right from the start I said there was no basis for this indictment. The trial has proved just that. The trial has proved conclusively that no crime was committed by myself, by my assistants, or by the police officers who searched the Black Panther apartment on December 4, 1969."

•

Said Mayor Daley: "The verdict speaks for itself. The great lesson here for all of us is not to be too willing to believe charges until there is a thorough airing of the facts. I think the black people of Chicago feel the same way. They want their streets to be safe."

•

Said Mrs. Emma Lee Garrett: "You know, to my feeling, I feel they would have found Hanrahan guilty, they would have let him went as guilty, you know, but for the sake of the law. To my feeling, they acquitted Hanrahan not guilty in order to uphold the law in Illinois."

TIME passes. It is winter now. Winter is everywhere in the air. Cold is in the air. The skies are flat and grey and hang low over the city, as they sometimes do in summer, but the little white boats are gone, and the girls in their short dresses are gone, and the music on the outdoor hamburger stands has stopped. Perhaps the sun now shines upon Australia and Brazil, but it rarely does here this time of year, and when it does it has not enough heat to warm the sidewalks, which are frozen, or thaw the great ugly brick buildings, which are frozen, or even bring memories of running and leaping and hot summer air to the people, who go about their business and their lives in overcoats and trouser cuffs rimmed with snow.

This is the North, after all. This is Kiev, and Warsaw,

and Bremerhaven, and Denmark, and the cold mist of the English midlands. Freezing hands and running noses in Hamburg and Cleveland. Nordic cities. Imagine life here without cities. Imagine the Indians camped beside Lake Michigan in the winter. Two nights ago, another of the great storms blew out of Canada, literally out of Canada, huge winds racing across the lake, piling up the water, freezing water cascading over the breakwaters, and howling cold wind whistling through the dark streets. Imagine being an Indian then. Or one of the first settlers hammering wood huts together on the mud. We live in an odd world, surely, when brick seems ugly, and stone seems cold and frozen.

Some things have happened here lately, although you would be hard put to see too many of the changes. There was a big fire atop the Hancock building, which was on the national TV news. A lot of broken glass which somehow didn't fall on anyone, and flames you could actually see from the street, ninety floors up. The firemen put it out in forty minutes. The firemen are not going on strike, but the police are talking about it. There is a dispute about a "work contract," or lack of one, and Mr. Daley and Superintendent Conlisk have been keeping busy attending to the matter. The Black Hawks are not doing so well this year, because Bobby Hull went off, or back, to Canada, and because of injuries. As the sports announcers say—in pro sports, injuries are the things to watch. A Chicago woman was killed in Los Angeles last week, no one knows why. Police are investigating. The other day, Mayor Daley, who is seventy years old and a grandfather, urged the City Council to ban unsafe toys from Chicago stores, which then passed a bill doing so, and Chicago area parents are certainly grateful for that.

In politics here, there have also been some developments. For one: Dan Walker, who kept saying he was an anti-Machine candidate, is now Governor Walker, who keeps saying he is an anti-Machine Governor, and maybe he will be. Governor Ogilvie, the upright Republican, who made the mistake of trying to unsnaffle the Cook County welfare rolls with upright Republican bookkeeping, is now ex-Governor Ogilvie.

For another: Edward Hanrahan is no longer State's Attorney for Cook County. He lost to Bernard Carey, the Republican ex-FBI man from the suburbs—not by many votes, to be sure, but still he (and the Democrats) lost the job and the office. This was a surprise, although more of a surprise to some than to others—and who knows what might have happened if Richard Nixon hadn't been running so strongly?

What apparently did happen is that the city's black wards—those wards which had been so carefully gerrymandered, and controlled, and organized, and precinct-captained, and had delivered for the white Democratic Machine time after time, election after election—finally wouldn't deliver for Hanrahan. They delivered for the judges, and the controller, and the clerk, and the small officials who mainly run the city, and to some slight degree for McGovern, but not for Hanrahan.

Hanrahan himself went into a post-partum rage in which he chivvied Mayor Daley for not having supported him enough, and talked moodily and vaguely about "fair-weather friends." The most coherent reason for

Carey's victory, though, is probably best supplied once again by Mrs. Emma Lee Garrett, citizen and voter. "Look here, twelve whole dollars!" she said the day after the election. "I guess I voted just about everywhere. Ten times at least. They took us around to different polling places in cars. Why, this money come on down, I don't know where from, where it always come from—from the Party, you know, from Hanrahan. But this time we all said: Now why should we vote for that Hanrahan? Why should we vote for *him?*"

The Machine presumably is still with us, but working in increasingly curious ways its wonders to perform: in this instance, distributing moneys to carloads of black housewives, chuffing along through the black wards of Chicago, emancipated finally neither by the politicians, *any* of them, nor by employment opportunities, nor by the Gospel, nor by subscriptions to *Ebony*, nor even by their cars which are forever breaking down, nor by anything except perhaps, for a few moments every few years, by the curtains and levers of the new voting machines—the recent purchase of which by a Cook County official (from somebody's close friend or brother-in-law) being, as it happens, the subject of yet another small ongoing scandal.

And so Hanrahan is out. At one point, he was considered Daley's heir as Mayor, and maybe when he re-emerges he will push himself toward the job. It will clearly take some pushing. "Eddie overplayed it," said one of his friends recently. "He never figured that Panther raid would blow up so big. He never had a chance to articulate himself to the black community."

One has the feeling, in the end, that Eddie Hanrahan did just that: he articulated himself—one of the last, perhaps, of the urban Irish-Catholic politicians, with one arm in front of him, waving a Harvard Law degree into the unclear future, but both feet in the clay of Irish-America behind him, with its old belligerences, and braggadocio, and fears, and ambitions, and Mother-of-God austerity. An ancient man in an ancient city—but an ancient city struggling, with the usual imperfections and self-deceptions, into the modern world, wherever that may be, leaving the few ancient men to turn madly in on themselves, or madly out on the enemy.

The enemy was there, wasn't he? Out on West Monroe Street? Or in the coloring books? Or now in the De Mau Mau catacombs? And Eddie Hanrahan had all the credentials to lead the fight: the old neighborhood, the good parochial school, splendid Notre Dame, Joe Kennedy's Harvard—and he had the right white-ethnic instinct on race, didn't he? Or did he? A week ago a reporter asked Bernard Carey, who seems a pleasant fair-minded man, also Irish-Catholic (the same high school as Mayor Daley), what he planned to do about street gangs. "I intend to fight crime not criminals," said Bernard Carey. A modern phrase. A modern man. Bernard Carey, one guesses, would not put black children into buses and send them to be educated in white schools, but nor would he (one guesses) serve vengeful search warrants on their older brothers at five in the morning.

Finally, perhaps it is *excess* that is nowadays most objectionable, even to liberals, and maybe even to blacks, although that is but another guess. Does it remind us too well of our dreadful past? Or does it simply not *work* in the human machinery of our new societies?—questions for another moment. In any case, modern men now, for modern times. There is small room any more for noisy primitives, for Goths and Gothic figures, for any violent brooding Ajax with any violent all-too-visible sword. And probably good riddance, too. Although sometimes it's hard to know nowadays, isn't it, just where the fight is. There *is* a fight now, isn't there? Or is there? It gets so quiet here sometimes—in Judge Romiti's courtroom, in Mayor Daley's city, in President Nixon's land. Some disturbances, of course, but when stones are thrown, they seem to become pebbles in the air, and land in cotton wool. Doubtless everything is in its place.

And out on West Monroe Street, things now are also much the same. In winter, none of Chicago is very lovely, except maybe Michigan Avenue where the big stores have their Christmas lights up, and the 2300 block on West Monroe is no exception. The colors on the outside of some of the houses are cheery enough, but there are a lot of broken windows everywhere, and a couple of the houses seem to have just been burned, set afire—maybe a stray Air Force bomb—and stand there. Mute testament to something or other, as Barnabas Sears might say.

This particular afternoon it is about four o'clock and there is virtually no one on the street, not the whole length of the 2300 block, except for a couple of men trying to start a car, and a man who has taken a stepladder outside on this cold afternoon and is painting or doing something to one of the windows of No. 2341, which is a three-story, brown brick building, with green trim on the windows.

Most of the houses on the block are red brick, three stories, several apartments to each story. Some of the houses have yellow trim on the windows, and others have green, and down the street on the next block there is a house done in a whole variety of greens—light green on the walls, and bright green on the front door, and a different green for the window trim and so forth. There are trees on the street, but the leaves are off them. A couple of old tires are tossed over a fire hydrant, maybe a game. There is litter everywhere, mostly paper lying in the streets and on the sidewalk. There is a garbage can on the corner stuffed to overflowing with trash. Cans of soda pop beneath the trees.

No. 2337 West Monroe is a house like any other on the block, except (as with its neighbor, 2339) the bricks are painted grey, and there is green trim around the windows, most of which are without glass, and some on the ground floor are boarded up. Broken wood stairs lead up to the front door, which is of wood, with paint splotches over it. There is an old mattress lying on the patch of dirt in front of the house, and at the top of the stairs, an old car seat, all springs and stuffing.

The two men who were trying to start the car have gone inside one of the other houses, and now return with a third man. None of them seems to be saying anything. The hood of the car is up. In the distance, far far off, like

Mont St. Michel, the mass of Chicago's tall buildings rise beside the water's edge. Snow is in the air. A dog barks, almost the first sound. Then two small children walk by— home from school.

In back of 2337, there is an alley running behind all the houses, and a yard of sorts, which is now fenced off and full of weeds and desolate grey grass, and another dog, who is gnawing on an old tire. The kitchen door is off the hinges and flaps open. Inside it is dark and strewn with paint peelings, and on the floor of the kitchen there is an old rusted stove, turned on its side, and an old rusted sink. The walls of the rooms and hallway are painted a dull kind of grey, except for the kitchen which is brown. It is all so very small, and so dingy. The bed-rooms—did Deborah Johnson and Fred Hampton cohabit, conceive a child, travel through the night together in that back bedroom? The room is barely big enough for a bed. The walls are full of bullet holes, which still have crayoned numbers beside each one, perhaps written there by Zimmers during his examination; and there is no space; and no light; and the ceiling seems to be right over the bed.

The whole apartment is like that. Tiny dingy rooms, and the ceiling low over one's head. Did Bobby Rush one afternoon phone Fred Hampton at work or in jail and say, "You'll never guess, I found the greatest apart-ment on West Monroe Street"? Nine people were living there. Nine people, mostly teenagers—did they argue, and wrangle, did they fight over toothpaste, and who took baths, and who used the reading lamp? Nine black revolutionaries, with their nerves frayed by paranoia, as well as by clear and present danger. Doubtless also it was fun sometimes, as war, especially guerrilla war, is said to be fun sometimes. Ingrid Bergman and Gary Cooper in *For Whom the Bell Tolls*. For Deborah Johnson and Fred Hampton on their mattress, before someone spilled chocolate stains all over it, did the earth move? Later, someone said that the mattress probably lifted right off the ground from the force of those machine gun bullets. Machine gun bullets in a warren. Chocolate stains.

And Fred Hampton? One remembers that Hampton was once sent to Menard State Prison in Joliet because he stole, or "liberated," popsicles from an ice cream truck and distributed them to children who were swarming around the truck. He must have had a certain amount of humor. At least, he must have been the sort of man who appreciates a good popsicle on a hot day. (It was this period in Menard State, they say, that changed him from a young NAACP worker to a radical-Red-Chinese-sympathizing troublemaker.) In any case, humor would probably have been a good thing to have going for one as a tenant in 2337 West Monroe, although it is said to be a quality that rarely goes well with revolution. The Irish have certainly produced their share of revolutionaries, but perhaps the humor is different.

Outside, through the front windows, the car is still not started, the hood is up, the men are gone. Across the street, the man on the stepladder still paints the window trim. Perhaps he is preparing for a Christmas light display the way they do downtown, or in the Mayor's neighborhood over in Bridgeport. Colored lights on all the houses.

And carols. And musical chimes which play Christmas music.

Out on the street again the wind has come up. Maybe another storm coming in across the lake. In movie scenes, newspapers blow softly down streets, calendar leaves tumble by. The papers here stay where they are. Some cans of Fanta. Diet-Rite. And bits and scraps of unidentified paper. No leaves on the trees. No people on the streets. There is a fairly large tree right in front of 2337, an elm. It looks in good shape, not yet succumbed to the Dutch Elm disease that has stripped so many other midwestern streets. Perhaps it looks better in spring. Most everything looks better in spring.

The man has climbed off the stepladder and is taking it back into the house. There is the sound of a door closing far down the street. On evenings like this, did Indians camp beside the lake—and what did they dream of? The cry of wolves? Problems of urban sprawl? Fish in a stream? Spring? The house on West Monroe Street is a house like any other there. An old row house, now getting older; the green paint, a lime shade, now flaking into other colors. Did something happen here? Was it important? Two schoolkids come walking back down the block—the same two, two little black girls. Earmuffs and mittens. Time passing everywhere. Time passes. Time.

AUTHOR'S NOTE

The following material was especially helpful in preparing this book: The *Report of the January 1970 Grand Jury* (U. S. District Court, Northern District of Illinois); the Report of the Goldberg–Clark "Commission of Inquiry"; and various research papers issued by the Chicago Law Enforcement Study Group, 1970, 1972.

ABOUT THE AUTHOR

Mr. Arlen was born in England in 1930 and came to this country during the Second World War. He was graduated from Harvard in 1952, worked as a reporter for *Life* for several years, and since then has been a staff writer for *The New Yorker*. His previous books are *Living-Room War* (1969) and *Exiles* (1970).

AN AMERICAN VERDICT

Was it a matter of murder? Or was it instead a result of standard law enforcement procedures against dangerous radicals? In December 1969, two members of the Black Panther Party were killed in Chicago, and several others wounded, by gunfire from a raiding party of police dispatched by the Cook County State's Attorney. The police said they had fired only in self-defense. The surviving Panthers said the two men had been murdered.

AN AMERICAN VERDICT is about the trial that eventually took place—of the Cook County State's Attorney and twelve policemen for "obstructing justice." It is about the original event —the police raid that took place on that now distant moment in the late 1960s. It is about Chicago—Mayor Daley's Chicago—"a particular American city

(continued on back flap)